Key History
for GCSE

Crime and Punishment
A study across time

Angela Anderson

Stanley Thornes (Publishers) Ltd

First published in 1998 by:
Stanley Thornes (Publishers) Ltd
Ellenborough House
Wellington Street
CHELTENHAM GL50 1YW
England

98 99 00 01 02 / 10 9 8 7 6 5 4 3 2 1

A catalogue record for this book is available from the British Library.

ISBN 0-7487-3057-5

Printed and bound in Italy by STIGE, Turin

Cover illlustration: Mansell Collection

Acknowledgements

Especial thanks are due to Dr Tim Lomas of the Lincolnshire Advisory Service for help in obtaining manor court records, and to Dr Roger Swift of Chester University College for sources and advice relating to nineteenth-century crime and policing. The author is grateful for their support and the more general guidance that they offered.

The author and publishers would like to thank the following for permission to reproduce photographs and other copyright materials in this book:

Charles Murray, for permission to reproduce extracts from the article 'Sentenced to a crime wave', *Sunday Times*, 5 January 1997.

b = bottom, t = top, l = left, r = right
AKG London, 4, 5
Ancient Art & Architecture Collection 12b, 15t
Bildarchiv Preussischer Kulturbesitz, 10,11, 12t
Bodleian Library, 42, 44
Bridgeman Art Library, London, 35b, 55
British Library Reproductions, 35t, 36, 39 (both), 46t
The Archbishop of Canterbury and the Trustees of Lambeth Palace Library, 38
English Heritage Photographic Library, 21
Mary Evans Picture Library, 15b, 20, 29, 43, 46b, 47, 48 (both), 51, 54, 58, 59 (both), 61, 62, 63, 67, 69, 73, 74, 76, 81, 84, 85 (both), 86, 87, 88, 91, 92 (both), 93, 97, 100
Mary Evans Picture Library/Fawcett Society, 95, 96, 98

The Fotomas Index, 52, 56, 64
Getty Images, 77, 90, 103r, 108, 109r
Gloucester Collection, 75t, 89l
Guildhall Library, Corporation of London, 50 (both)
Historical Newspaper Loan Service, 99
By Courtesy of the National Portrait Gallery, London, 78, 89r
Rex Features, 101, 105, 107, 111
Royal Collection Enterprises, 41
By Courtesy of the Trustees of Sir John Soane's Museum, 70
Tate Gallery London, 94
Telegraph Colour Library, 109l
Master and Fellows of Trinity College, Cambridge, 33
Wellcome Centre Medical Photographic Library, 103l
Roger Wood, 18
City of York Libraries, 83

The publishers have been unable to trace the copyright holders of the pictures on pages 30, 45, 53, 65 and 75 (Source D), and would be pleased to receive any information which would enable them to do so, in order to make the necessary arrangements.

Every effort has been made to contact copyright holders. The publishers apologise to anyone whose rights have been inadvertently overlooked, and will be happy to rectify any errors or omissions.

Contents

1 **The earliest written laws** *4*

2 **Law, crime and punishment in the Roman Empire** *6*

Roman government and society under the Republic *6*
Roman government and society under the Empire *8*
Roman law *10*
Case File: The law of the Twelve Tables *14*
Roman law and punishment in practice *16*
Case File: Race and justice in Roman Britain *19*

3 **The development of the English legal system** *22*

The invasions of Britain *22*
Anglo-Saxon law *24*
Enforcing Anglo-Saxon law *26*
Enforcing Norman law *28*

4 **The evolution of English law** *30*

Henry II and the restoration of the legal system *30*
Later developments *32*

5 **Crime, society and religion** *34*

6 **Law and the people in late medieval England** *36*

Justice and injustice *36*
Case File: The Peasants' Revolt of 1381 *38*

7 **Crime and punishment, 1500–1750** *40*

Overview *40*
The enforcement of law *42*
Improving law enforcement *44*

8 **Crime and society, 1500–1750** *46*

Poverty and disorder *46*
Crime, poverty and the poor laws *48*
London: a criminal underworld *50*

9 **Crime and religion, 1500–1750** *54*

The early Tudors and the Church *54*
The Church and the persecution of Catholics *56*
Case File: The Gunpowder Plot *58*
Crime and superstition: witches and witchcraft *60*
The development of religious freedom *63*

10 **Crime and protest, 1500–1750** *64*

11 **Crime and society in the eighteenth century** *66*

12 **Crime and punishment into the twentieth century** *68*

13 **The need for reform, 1750–1820** *70*

Patterns of crime *70*
The Bloody Code *72*
Popular protest, 1750–1820 *74*
Case File: The Peterloo Massacre, 1819 *76*

14 **An age of reform, 1820–1950** *78*

The coming of reform *78*
The early police force *80*
Local police forces *82*
Police and public order *84*
Crime and criminals *86*
Changes in punishment *88*
Prison reform *91*
Women and crime *94*
Case File: The Suffragettes *96*

15 **Crime and punishment since 1950: a changing world** *100*

Overview *100*
Crime since 1950 *102*
Evidence about crime *104*
Punishment since 1950 *106*
Capital punishment *108*
Policing in modern Britain *110*

Index *112*

1 The earliest written laws

Laws in the ancient world

 When were the first laws laid down? What were they?

All societies need laws, and there is evidence that laws have existed from the earliest times. The laws define what is a crime, and what punishment should be applied. The sources here are examples of written laws, the earliest written down more than 4,000 years ago, but written laws were usually based on customs that had been established even earlier. Why do you think people took the trouble to write down their laws if people were already used to them?

The law code of Hammurabi

The earliest code, shown in Source **A**, was written on the orders of Hammurabi, king of Babylon (in what is now Iraq) around 2100 BC. The code contains 284 laws, some of which are listed in Source **B**. They cover every aspect of life, from crimes such as theft and murder, through family relationships, damage to property, debt, the position and treatment of slaves, and even rates of pay. It reveals a complex and wealthy society, made up of different ranks and classes. In contrast, the Ten Commandments shown in Source **C** were given to a nomadic people, who probably lived by herding sheep and goats, in the process of migrating to a new land. How do the two law codes (Sources **B** and **C**) reflect the differences between the two societies? Do they have anything in common?

Source A One of the carved pillars on which Hammurabi's laws were inscribed. The pillar is now in the Louvre Museum in Paris, France.

Source B Extracts from the laws of Hammurabi – the world's oldest law code

1 If a man has laid a curse upon another man, and it is not justified, the layer of the curse shall be slain …
3 If in a lawsuit a man gives damnatory evidence, and his word that he has spoken is not justified, then if the suit be a capital one [i.e. if the case is one of murder], that man shall be slain.
4 If he has given evidence concerning corn or silver, then whatever the penalty of the lawsuit, he shall suffer it …
8 If a man has stolen an ox, or a sheep, or an ass, or a pig, or a boat either from a god or a palace, he shall pay thirty-fold. If he is a plebeian [a commoner], he shall render ten-fold. If the thief has nothing to pay, he shall be slain …
117 If a man has contracted a debt, and has given his wife, his son, his daughter for silver or for labour, three years they shall serve in the house of their purchaser or bondsmaster; in the fourth year they shall regain their original condition …
127 If a man has pointed a finger against a priestess or the wife of another man unjustifiably, that man shall be thrown before the judge, and his brow shall be branded …
129 If the wife of a man is found lying with another male, they shall be bound and thrown into the water; unless the husband lets his wife live and the king lets his servant live …
195 If a son has struck his father, his hands shall be cut off.
196 If a man has destroyed the eye of a free man, his own eye shall be destroyed … if he has broken the bone of a free man, his bone shall be broken …
209 If a man strike the daughter of a free man, and cause her foetus to fall, he shall pay ten shekels of silver for her foetus … If that woman die, his daughter shall be slain …

The Ten Commandments

The Ten Commandments were given to the Jews on their journey out of Egypt to find the promised land of Israel, probably around 1225 BC. Moses, their leader, brought them down from Mount Sinai, carved on two stone tablets, and presented them to the people as the basis of their law (see Source **D**). The commandments were said to have been dictated by God himself. Source **E** is further evidence of the link between law and religion in the ancient world.

Source C   The Ten Commandments

1 And God spoke all these words:
2 'I am the Lord your God, who brought you out of Egypt, out of the land of slavery.
3 'You shall have no other gods before me.
4 'You shall not make for yourself an idol in the form of anything in heaven above or on the earth beneath or in the waters below ...
7 'You shall not misuse the name of the Lord your God ...
8 'Remember the Sabbath day by keeping it holy ...
12 'Honour your father and your mother ...
13 'You shall not murder.
14 'You shall not commit adultery. **15** 'You shall not steal.
16 'You shall not give false testimony against your neighbour.
17 'You shall not covet your neighbour's house ... or anything that belongs to your neighbour.'

From Exodus 20:1–17, New International Version

Source D   Moses and the Ten Commandments

When laws restrained mankind from open violence, but men did hidden wrong, then I think some ingenious man put forward the notion that there were gods to fear, so that evildoers might be afraid even if their actions and words and thoughts were hidden.

Source E   From a speech by Kritias, a character in a Greek play of the fifth century BC

Questions

1 What crimes are listed in Sources **B** and **C**? Which of these would be considered crimes today?

2 What crimes are mentioned in *both* Source **B** *and* Source **C**? Would they all be considered crimes today?

3 List five modern crimes which would not be mentioned in these law codes. Why not?

4 Using your answers to questions 1–3, explain how crime has changed. What elements of continuity can you see between ancient and modern crime?

5 What do sources **C** and **E** suggest about the relationship between law and religion?

6 What sorts of punishment were used in Source **B**? What do you think they were trying to achieve?

7 In what ways are modern punishments different? Are there any similarities?

8 Using the sources and your answers to questions 1–7, explain in your own words: **a)** What is crime? **b)** What is the aim of punishment? **c)** Why do societies need law?

2 Law, crime and punishment in the Roman Empire

Roman government and society under the Republic

▶ *How did Roman government and society develop?*

The origins of Rome

The city of Rome developed at the end of the Bronze Age (*c.* 1000 BC) from settlements clustered around the lowest crossing-point of the River Tiber, and its earliest inhabitants were farmers who built strongholds on the hills around the river. Early Roman society consisted of three tribes which were sub-divided into families and clans. The head of the family (*paterfamilias*) seems to have held great power over his wife and children. It was a closely knit society linked by a system of clientship (*clientela*) in which the richer families took responsibility for helping the poorer, and expected some personal loyalty in return. The relationship passed from generation to generation.

Tribes were governed by a king, with the help of an Assembly, which made laws and conducted trials. The earliest assemblies were based on the three tribes, with probably 300 elected members, but the system was reorganised in the early sixth century by King Servius (died 525 BC), who divided the people into four city and seventeen rural tribes. The voting system gave greatest influence to the city tribes and the wealthiest families. About a thousand of these families probably made up the *patrician* class, who took over the government when the last king, Tarquin the Proud, was driven out in about 510 BC.

The establishment of the Republic

The new form of government was a Republic – a government without a king. Its structure is shown in Source **A**. This developed further in the fifth and fourth centuries BC, when the *plebeians* (the mass of citizens, as opposed to the patricians) set up the office of the Tribunes of the People and a Plebeian Council. But the structure of the Republic and the client system combined to ensure that it was run by the wealthy families and the patrician class.

MAGISTRATES WHO GOVERNED

Two Consuls:
• ran the city
• chief military leaders
• limited only by law
• elected for one year only, then rejoined Senate

Other magistrates included:
• Censors
• Aediles
• Quaestors
• Praetors (see below)
• Tribunes (see below)
Magistracies open to plebeians, and ex-magistrates went to Senate

Praetors (8 at end of Republic):
• chief magistrates when Consuls were on campaign
• administered the law
Praetor Urbanus ('of the city'), from 366 BC
Praetor Peregrinus ('over foreigners'), from 242 BC

Tribunes (10):
• expressed views of plebeians
• called and ran Plebeian Council
Started as representative of plebeians; later became part of establishment

The conquest of Italy

To defend itself against former rulers and rival tribes in Italy such as the Sabines and the Samnites, Rome made alliances with other cities which shared the Latin culture. As its population grew, Rome needed more land. The success of the citizen army allowed the Senate to establish new colonies (settlements) of citizens and soldiers and establish a defensive ring around the city (see Source **B**).

Rome's Italian allies were able to see that Roman citizenship offered special status and benefits. Some wealthy Latins were granted citizenship, but the Senate would not admit large numbers of non-Roman voters. In the fourth century BC the Senate granted half-citizenship, consisting of legal rights but not the right to vote, to the Latin cities and peoples. Some other peoples were allies who relied on Roman protection and therefore had to accept Roman decisions. As Roman power grew, this pattern was repeated over large areas of Italy and defence turned into expansion. By the end of the Samnite Wars in the early third century BC, Rome controlled virtually the whole Italian peninsula.

GOVERNING BODIES

People's Assembly

In theory ruled Rome, but voting weighted according to wealth and in practice controlled by the Senate

- elected senior magistrates
- made laws
- passed death penalty
- declared war and peace

Senate

In theory advised the Assembly, but:
- nominated consuls
- experienced in government and the army
- made up of rich and powerful citizens, patrons of 'clients'
So in practice they controlled the Assembly

Plebeian Council

Started from popular meetings to express discontent; formally set up from 471 BC

- elected plebeian Tribunes and Aediles
- held trials for non-capital offences
- from 287 BC decisions (*plebiscites*) made legally binding, equal to those of the Assembly

Source A The structure of the Roman Republic

Overseas conquest and rule

Power and overseas trade brought contact with new friends and enemies. Rivalry with Greek colonies in Italy led to war and victory against Greek and Macedonian kings. In Africa Rome had a long struggle against Carthage, which made Rome a major power in the Mediterranean and North Africa. Conquered enemies became client kings, or their lands were made into Roman *provinces* (countries governed by Rome). Generals rewarded their troops by establishing new Roman colonies in the lands they had conquered. In 90 BC a rebellion among the Italian allies forced the Senate to grant full citizenship to all Italians in the following year, but Rome was by then the centre of a growing empire. In 27 BC the Republic ended after a long civil war, and government was taken into the hands of Augustus, the first emperor.

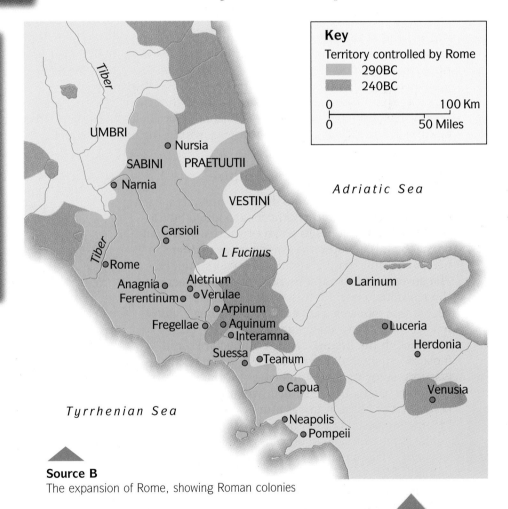

Key

Territory controlled by Rome

- 290BC
- 240BC

0 ———— 100 Km
0 ———— 50 Miles

Source B

The expansion of Rome, showing Roman colonies

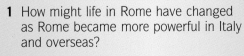

Questions

1 How might life in Rome have changed as Rome became more powerful in Italy and overseas?

2 Why do you think being a Roman citizen was important?

7

Roman government and society under the Empire

▶ *How was Roman government and society organised under the Empire ?*

The Roman Empire ruled much of Europe for four hundred years, (27 BC–AD 476) and the eastern Mediterranean for a thousand years. Throughout this time its basic structure remained similar. Source **A** shows the way the Empire was governed.

The emperor

At the head of the Empire was the emperor. He ruled with the help of a Senate and a council of advisers, but his decisions were final. When he died he became a god, so that worship of the emperors was added to the existing religious cults in Rome. It was for this reason that Christians were persecuted in Rome, because as they believed that there was only one God they were considered to be disloyal. The emperor could choose his successor, and this led to vicious plots and intrigues within the imperial court.

The organisation of the Empire

The Empire was divided into different provinces, each with a governor and other officers appointed by the emperor or the Senate. Imperial provinces (where the emperor himself chose the governor) were often nearer the frontiers where the army was stationed. The governor was a military ruler and a member of the senatorial class; he was assisted by a *procurator*, who was responsible for taxation and finance. Both reported directly to the emperor.

Although the Empire covered a huge area, and most of its population were farmers, its character was formed by its towns and cities, each a small version of Rome itself. Planned, well-ordered and policed (they often began as army camps), they became increasingly wealthy and beautified by fine public buildings. Roman officials encouraged the spread of Roman culture. This included the building of public baths and amphitheatres, and Roman games. The Empire was administered by an efficient imperial bureaucracy, held together by a network of roads that allowed rapid communication and by the power of the imperial army. At its head the emperor maintained tight control. The result across the Empire was the *pax romana* ('the Roman peace').

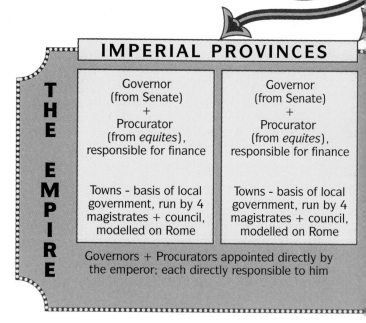

The importance of citizenship

Roman citizenship carried legal rights and a special status which made it highly valued by anyone who had to live under Roman power, and granting citizenship helped to make sure people stayed loyal. Half-citizenship was also used to enable more men to become eligible for the army. This system allowed Roman culture and influence to expand in a way that was appropriate to each situation and new area.

Later emperors were not born in Rome, or even in

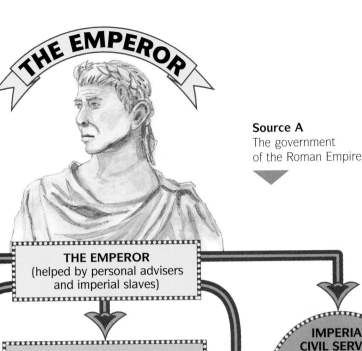

THE EMPEROR

Source A
The government
of the Roman Empire

THE EMPEROR
(helped by personal advisers
and imperial slaves)

THE SENATE
• made laws as the emperor wished
• chose magistrates
(Consuls, Praetors) from the
emperor's nominees
• magistrates later served as
provincial governors and then
returned to the Senate

**IMPERIAL
CIVIL SERVICE**
• responsible for
administration and taxes
• dominated by the
class of knights (*equites*)
• individual knights
served as provincial
Procurators

An unequal society

Citizenship did not necessarily mean that society
became more just. Society was rigidly divided into
two classes. The city-state had patricians and
plebeians, and the Empire distinguished between
the wealthy middle and upper classes who
administered the state (the *honestiores*) and
the masses of free residents (the *humiliores*).
By AD 212, one's influence and quality of
life, and even the application of the law,
depended on one's class rather than race
or citizenship. Society in the Roman
Empire was often well governed
but never democratic or equal.

ENATORIAL PROVINCES

Governor
(from Senate)
+
Quaestor
(from Senate),
ponsible for taxes

ns - basis of local
ernment, run by 4
istrates + council,
odelled on Rome

Governor
(from Senate)
+
Quaestor
(from Senate),
responsible for taxes

Towns - basis of local
government, run by 4
magistrates + council,
modelled on Rome

ernors chosen in the Senate, but ultimately
onsible to the emperor; Quaestors directly
responsible to him

IMPERIAL PROVINCES

Governor
(from Senate)
+
Procurator
(from *equites*),
responsible for finance

Towns - basis of local
government, run by 4
magistrates + council,
modelled on Rome

Governor
(from Senate)
+
Procurator
(from *equites*),
responsible for finance

Towns - basis of local
government, run by 4
magistrates + council,
modelled on Rome

Augustus made sure that border provinces, with
a strong army presence, were imperial provinces,
while senatorial provinces were older and more
established. Why do you think he did this?

THE EMPIRE

Italy, and the imperial civil service contained men
from many backgrounds, including non-Roman
citizens, the emperor's personal slaves and ex-slaves
or their descendants. The army continued to provide
a continuing source of new citizens, since military
service was automatically rewarded with citizenship
and a grant of land on retirement. When the emperor
Caracalla granted citizenship to all free subjects of
the Empire in AD 212, it completed Rome's transition
from Republican city-state to multinational Empire.

Questions

1 How did Roman government and
society change following the growth of
Roman power and a vast empire?

2 Using all the information on pp. 6–9, say how
these changes might have affected crime,
punishment and the law.

Roman law

> *Why is Roman law so important? How was it made?*

Law and justice

Crime and punishment in Rome were both defined by laws, which set out what actions were considered crimes, and how they were to be punished.

Roman law developed over a thousand years. Laws were codified (collected and revised in written form) by legal experts at various times in Rome's history, the most comprehensive codification being that of the emperor Justinian in AD 529–34 (see Source **A**).

Source A   What is law?

Anyone intending to study law [*ius*, or *jus*] should first know whence the word *ius* is derived. It was named *ius* from *justice*; for, as Celsus [a Roman scholar and writer] aptly defined it, law is the act of the good and the fair … Justice is the constant and perpetual will to give each man his right.

From the *Digest* of Justinian, AD 533

As Source **B** suggests, Roman law was a huge achievement which provided the foundation of law in Europe; it established fundamental beliefs about what law should be and its relationship to justice. But people were not always treated fairly in Rome. We therefore need to consider three important questions:

- How did Roman law change and develop, from rules for a small city-state to a legal code for an empire?
- Did Roman law really aim to provide justice?
- Did it provide justice for all, regardless of who they were and where they came from?

After studying the sources in the rest of this chapter, you should be able to answer these questions.

Source B   The achievement of Roman law

The greatest achievement of the Romans, whether we consider it on its own merits or in its influence on the history of the world, is without doubt, their law … Whereas the population of the Roman Empire may have been 50 millions, at present, 870 million people live under systems traceable to Roman law.

From R.H. Barrow, *The Romans*, 1949

Early Roman law and the Twelve Tables

The Assembly had the right to pass legislation (formal laws) and conduct trials, but the wealthier you were, the more voting power you had. During the fifth century BC a Plebeian Council was established, run by the Tribunes, and in 287 BC its decisions were declared to be equal to those of the Assembly – but even there, voting was weighted in favour of the wealthier plebeians. Thus, formal law was always in the hands of the upper classes.

Ordinary citizens needed to know their legal rights, and this led to demands for the laws to be written down. One particular problem was the harsh laws on debt, which allowed a debtor and his children to be sold into slavery if a debt was unpaid. Pressure from the plebeians finally led to the appointment of a commission in 451 BC which recorded the existing laws on stone tablets. These Twelve Tables formed the basis of Roman law. (See the Case File on pp. 14–15.)

Source C   The Roman Forum, showing the senate house. The Assembly and the Plebeian Council met in the space in front of the senate house.

Consuls and praetors

The Romans also realised that law needed to adapt to changing circumstances. Roman magistrates could issue laws to deal with new problems as they arose. The chief magistrates were the *consuls*, who often tried to deal with particular problems during their period of office. For example, the consul Poetelius reformed the laws on debt in 326 BC, by encouraging property rather than person to be provided as security for loans.

The most important magistrate for the development of law in the Republic was the *praetor* (see Sources **D** and **E**). Created in 366 BC, this office took over the administration of law in Rome. Praetors were elected for one year at a time, and issued edicts stating the aspects of law they would cover and what principles they would apply. So the praetors built up records of actual cases and also established legal principles; in effect they were adding to existing laws. Special praetors arranged how the law was applied to foreigners. They created a new kind of Roman law, the *ius gentium*, or 'law of nations'.

In the provinces, the law was applied by a provincial governor. Under the Republic he was responsible to the Senate, under the Empire to the emperor. At the beginning of his period in office, he usually issued an edict saying how he would interpret and apply the laws, as Source **F** describes.

The emperor Augustus reorganised the legal system, so that the Senate was used to pass the laws that the emperor required. At the same time the emperor could make law himself, and as the Empire developed emperors used their power as they chose. So law came to be made by the will of the emperor. It was fortunate, therefore, that the emperors were guided by established legal principles and a tradition of natural law and equity.

rce D
praetor

Source E The importance of the praetor

The praetor was above the law. The Praetor Peregrinus had to deal with foreigners not bound by Roman law; his task was to create out of the customs of Romans and the customs of foreigners a law acceptable to both ... it had to satisfy men as men, not men as citizens of this or that state. The Praetor Urbanus thus built up the law of citizens (*ius civile*); the Praetor Peregrinus built up the 'law of the nations' (*ius gentium*). As more and more cases involved both, the civil law gradually became more like the wider law of the nations.

From R.H. Barrow, *The Romans*, 1949

Source F The provincial governor

Meantime, the provincial governor also issued his edict to run in his province. He had held office in Rome, and he knew something of law. He studied the edict of his predecessor, and modified it in the light of his experience. He had to take into account local custom and prejudice, the habits of mind of his provincials; yet Roman notions of law and order must prevail. And, when he came back to take his place in the Senate, his experience was worth much.

From R.H. Barrow, *The Romans*, 1949

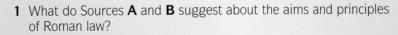

Questions

1 What do Sources **A** and **B** suggest about the aims and principles of Roman law?

2 Why was it such an important achievement?

3 What part was played in the development of Roman law by:
   • Roman citizens; • Roman magistrates; • the Roman emperor?

4 What evidence suggests that the aim of Roman law was to provide justice?

The Roman legal system in practice

A court case began when someone making the complaint went to the praetor who decided if the case was valid. Some crimes, like murder, could be settled by payment to the victim, but if there was no such settlement the praetor involved a law court (see Source **G**), with jury drawn from the patrician class. These became specialised in dealing with particular types of crimes. In 122 BC the *equites* (wealthier plebeians) were allowed to participate, and eventually cases of corruption of magistrates were administered solely by *equites*. Cases were presented by a trained orator (see Source **H**) who was skilled in speaking rather than in the law.

Legal advice was limited at first to the patricians, through their control of magistrates' offices, the courts and the order of priests (who also provided legal advice). In 300 BC, however, Appius Claudius allowed his secretary Flavius to publish the correct legal procedure. From about 253 BC the chief priest, Tiberius Coruncanius, began to admit students to his legal consultations, and this led to the development of legal training schools and of professional jurists or jurisprudents. They advised all parties concerned and it was their judgements that made up a growing body of case law.

Source G
The law court at Pompeii as it looks today

Source H Relief of a Roman orator

12

The codification of Roman law

As the Empire developed into an absolute monarchy the jurists preserved the principles of natural law and justice, partly through their advice, but also through written works. In the reigns of the emperors Hadrian and Marcus Aurelius, in the second century AD, much of this case law was collected and summarised by Salvius Julianus, and his pupil Gaius. Thereafter there were regular codifications of the law. Five great jurists were singled out as being of particular importance – Papinian, Paulus, Gaius, Ulpian and Modestinus. Ultimately, the laws were collated, summarised and refined in the great law codes of Theodosius (AD 438) and Justinian (AD 529–34), as Source **J** explains.

Source J   The codification of Roman law

It is of great value to us, for it gives a picture of the activities of the Christian emperors, and of the social conditions of the day. When barbarian races overran the West, and Italy was subject to foreign government, the barbarians incorporated into their own legal codes great masses of Roman law. The great codification was that of Justinian ... It included imperial statutes, and it also distilled the writings of the jurists; what was obsolete was omitted, and the whole was arranged in magnificent order. Justinian claimed that 3 million lines of law had been reduced to the 150,000 of the Digest.

From R.H. Barrow, *The Romans*, 1949

Natural law

As the Roman Empire expanded, the increasingly multicultural nature of legal cases meant that jurists had to rely on a sense of equity, and simple common sense. Greek influences encouraged an interaction between Greek and Roman civilisations, and by the first century BC the idea of natural law was firmly established, as Source **I** explains.

Source I   The acceptance of natural law

For Cicero [the famous late Republican orator], despite all his faults and the faults of his age, had accepted the Greek idea, now current among Roman jurists and other thinkers, of a Natural Law which ... ought to be observed by all mankind. That is to say, he was convinced that right is right and wrong is wrong objectively, and that no ... laws can make them otherwise. And what was most wrong of all, he believed, was for one person to tyrannise over others.

From M. Grant, *History of Rome*, 1978

The Roman Empire was already collapsing in the face of invasions, but the principles of Roman law would live on. As Source **J** shows, some Roman law passed into the codes of the new barbarian kingdoms and, in turn, provided the basic principles of law in later European nations such as France, Italy and Scotland. English law developed differently. The influence of Rome also lasted in Eastern Europe through the Byzantine Empire, which survived after the collapse of Roman power in the West.

Questions

1 What part was played in the development of Roman law by:
   a) the idea of natural law; **b)** the jurists?

2 Why has Roman law been of such lasting importance in Europe?

The law of the Twelve Tables

What do the Twelve Tables tell us about early Roman law?

Context and content

In the fifth century BC the legal framework of Rome was revised and recorded on twelve stone tablets, which were set up in the Roman Forum for all to see. These laws became the basis of all subsequent Roman law. Source **A** discusses their range and importance. Source **B** lists their contents.

Source A   The impact of the Twelve Tables

The impact of the Twelve Tables upon later generations was enormous ... The contents of the Tables form a strange mixture of widely ranging principles and minor details, of law private and public and criminal, of rules about matters from communal hygiene to personal safety ... It seems impressive that a people at such an early stage of development were so clearly able to disentangle law from religion ... not deriving the power of their laws from any divine or mythical lawgiver, but from a sense of justice and equity, still narrow yet already strong ...

From M. Grant, *History of Rome*, 1978

Source B   The contents of the Twelve Tables

Table 1 How to summon a man before the magistrates

Table 2 Rules for bail and calling witnesses

Table 3 Laws on debt

Tables 4 and 5 Family law

Tables 6 and 8 Property and ownership

Table 7 Building regulations

Table 9 Public law; crimes against the state

Table 10 Sacred law: mainly regulations regarding the conduct of funerals

Tables 11 and 12 Extra items from all the previous subjects

The laws in detail

Source **C** describes the laws on debt. The debtor is the person who owes money; the creditor is the person to whom he owes it; the plaintiff is the person bringing the case. Captivity could last sixty days, during which time the debtor had to be brought to the magistrates on three successive market days. Thereafter, if the debt was not paid, he could be put to death or sold as a slave 'to any stranger resident beyond the Tiber'. If there were several creditors, the body (or its value) would be divided.

Source C   Extract from the laws on debt

In case of debt either upon confession or judgement, the debtor shall have thirty days grace. That term having expired, the plaintiff can bring the debtor before the magistrate. If the debt is not paid, or surety provided, the creditor shall take the debtor, put him into chains or into the stocks, the weight of the chains not to exceed 15 pounds, but less at the creditor's will. The debtor shall be at liberty to live as he thinks fit, provided it be at his own expense. In the event of his being unable to provide his own nourishment [i.e. while in this captivity], the creditor in whose custody he is shall supply him with at least one pound of bread daily.

As Sources **D** and **E** show, Roman fathers had considerable powers over their family. Source **F** shows how laws protected person, property and reputation against damage, often with the severest penalties. The Tarpeian Rock (Source **G**) is a steep cliff near the Roman Forum from which murderers, traitors and other wrongdoers were flung to their deaths when convicted of a capital crime. In fact, only the Assembly could pass laws requiring the death penalty, and anyone convicted on such laws had a right of appeal. The death penalty was used for:
- homicide (the murder of a man)   •   arson
- libellers and public defamers   •   false witness
- a judge or arbitrator who accepted a bribe
- the use of spells and enchantments, or poisonous drugs
- attending seditious meetings by night in the city
- anyone who incited the enemy against Rome
- certain kinds of theft or fraud.

Source D Relief of a Roman family

Source F Extracts from the laws on damage to persons, property and reputations

Retaliation against he who breaks the limb of another and does not offer compensation.
- For the fracture of a bone (or a tooth) of a freeman, the penalty is 300 *asses*; in the case of a slave, 150. For any injury whatsoever committed upon another, 25 *asses*.
- For damage caused by a quadruped, reparation [payment or making good] or the forefeiture [surrender] of the animal.
- Capital punishment is decreed for libellers and public defamers.
- False witnesses to be thrown from the Tarpeian Rock.
- The incendiary of a house or of a haystack near a house, if acting intentionally and of sound mind, shall be bound, scourged and put to death by fire. If by negligence, he shall repair the damage, or, if too poor, shall be chastised moderately.

Source G The Roman criminal Cassius being thrown from the Tarpeian Rock

Source E Extracts from the laws on the family and the rights of the father

The father has the right to immediately destroy deformed offspring.
- The father has the right over his children, existing during their whole life, to imprison, scourge [whip], keep to agricultural labour in chains, to sell or slay, even though they may be in the enjoyment of high state offices.
- Three consecutive sales of the son by the father releases the son from his father's power.
- Women are to be kept in permanent tutelage. [A tutor was a legal guardian.]
- The testament [will] of the father is law regarding his property and control of it.
- A husband has marital power over his wife (and her property) by the fact of possession of one year – but this may be avoided if she absents herself for three nights consecutively in each year from the house of her husband.

Questions

1 What crimes did Roman law have to deal with?

2 Which punishments were aimed at: **a)** deterring criminals; **b)** revenge or retribution; and **c)** compensating victims?

3 Why was such extensive use made of the death penalty?

4 What evidence suggests that a good name or reputation was important? Why do you think this was so?

5 What evidence is there of any principles of equity (fairness) being applied in these punishments?

6 In what ways might these laws be considered harsh or unfair?

7 What kind of society were they intended to create? (Give examples to support your answer.)

Roman law and punishment in practice

▶ *Did Roman law provide justice?*

The importance of status

Although Roman laws seem impressive and comprehensive you must remember that they did not apply to everyone equally. They only applied to citizens, slaves had no rights and freedmen (ex-slaves) had only limited rights. Also, among the citizens themselves, some were privileged. Roman fathers had extensive rights; women had some rights, for example in owning property, but they were always treated as inferior in law.

The fairness of any law is always dependent on the way that it is applied and enforced, and the sources below show how this varied in Rome. Sources **A** to **C** show how a person's status could affect his or her legal rights in practice. Status could also affect the kind of punishment applied, as Source **D** shows.

Source A The freedman. (Civil suits were disputes between citizens, especially over property; criminal suits were those between a citizen and the State.)

The freedman must not act to the harm of his patron. He might bring civil suits against him only by permission of the authorities, and 'infaming actions' [which damage their good name and character] not at all; and the only criminal proceedings he might initiate against a patron were for treason.

From J.A. Crook, *Law and Life of Rome,* 1967

Source B The slave

Does Rutilius believe that slaves are the same as their masters? Not on your life! Nothing pleases him more than a good flogging. He loves the crack of the lash. He's a monster to his household. He's never so happy as when some poor slave who has stolen a couple of towels is being branded with red-hot irons. His chief pleasures are dungeons, burnt flesh and field labour camps.

Written by the poet Juvenal, in AD 110

Source C Women and children

Our children whom we have begotten in lawful wedlock are in our power. The power which we have over our children is peculiar to Roman citizens, and is found in no other nation. The offspring, then, of you and your wife is in your power, and so too is that of your son and his wife ... But the offspring of your daughter is not in your power, but in that of its own father. Women are in the power of their husbands, or if they have none, of their fathers. They are subject to guardianship, or tutelage.

From the *Institutes* of Justinian, AD 533

Source D Laws on adultery and forgery (*lex* = 'law')

The lex Julia, passed for the repression of adultery, punishes with death not only defilers of the marriage-bed, but also those who indulge in criminal intercourse with those of their own sex, and inflicts penalties on any who, without using violence, seduce virgins or widows of respectable character. If the seducer be of reputable condition, the punishment is the confiscation of half his fortune; if a mean person, flogging and relegation.

The lex Cornelia on forgery (of wills or other documents) inflicts penalties thus: if the criminal be a slave, the penalty fixed by statute is death, as in the statutes relating to assassins and poisoners; if a free man, deportation.

From the *Institutes* of Justinian, AD 533

Source F Some of the different punishments under Roman law ▶

The importance of wealth

Roman magistrates had the right to punish offenders without trial, and often did so. If the accused person denied the charge, the magistrate had to consult his advisors, and if they found him guilty, he was punished accordingly. In the case of important citizens, this process came under the control of the praetor, and went to a jury court, but poorer citizens were dealt with by lesser magistrates, the *tresviri* ('three men'). Their powers were extensive and severe, as described in Source **E**.

Source E The powers of magistrates under the Republic

The Twelve Tables proved inadequate as Rome developed into a large city with powerful social tensions. There thus arose, during the third century BC, a drastic police power, directed against those who were guilty of violence, arson, poisoning and theft. All of these were liable to the death penalty … In the last century of the Republic, the death penalty was, so far as can be seen, no longer carried out on those who belonged to the upper classes (*honestiores*); the magistrate allowed them to escape into exile. But slaves and criminals from the *humiliores* [lower classes], condemned for a capital offence by the police-court of the *tresviri*, were doubtless put to death.

From W. Kunkel, *Roman Legal and Constitutional History*, 1966

As the Empire developed the *tresviri* were replaced by the urban prefects, who exercised the same kind of powers. Wealthy citizens might be tried by the Senate, by the emperor himself or by the provincial governor, but the ordinary criminal had no access to this system. This distinction between the *honestiores* and the *humiliores* became more rigid. Some historians have argued that punishment also became harsher at this time.

Certainly, poor people who could not pay fines were made into slaves or given an effective death sentence as a gladiator. There was probably also a greater use of crucifixion, burning or being thrown to the animals in the games. There is some debate about how much change actually occurred. There had always been different treatment for patricians and the lower classes. The harsher sentences may reflect the growing number of foreigners in Rome and the Empire, who were always subject to worse penalties. But as the Empire developed these differences evolved into separate penalties according to status. When Caracalla granted citizenship to all free men in the Empire in AD 212, the two categories of citizen, the *honestiores* and the *humiliores*, were almost governed by two categories of law.

Questions

1 List the categories of people who would find it hard to get justice in Rome, and the reasons for their problems.

2 Look at the punishments illustrated in Source **F**. What crimes, and what kinds of criminals, might they apply to?

Other problems in Roman law

As well as the distinctions that were made according to your wealth or status, practical problems prevented the law from operating equally. Court cases required the services of an orator and the advice of jurists, which was inevitably expensive. In addition, many punishments could be reduced by payment of money to the victim or family, if they agreed. The law could be also be abused, as described in Source **G**.

Source G Abusing the system

Governors often condemn people to be held in prison or kept in chains, but they are not supposed to do so, for such penalties are forbidden; prisons ought to be for detaining men [for trial], not for punishing them.

From the *Institutes* of Justinian, AD 533

Corrupt or bad judgement was not uncommon. Source **H** is the orator Cicero's famous description of Verres, the governor of Sicily. Corruption could occur at any level, but the wealthy had more chance of dealing with it. The urban prefects of the Empire were trained professionals and probably an improvement on earlier magistrates. Their justice was often swift and effective but they could be influenced by powerful interests and by society's attitudes and prejudices regarding class, race and religion.

Source H Verres, the corrupt governor of Sicily

In Sicily, during those three years, not a single lawsuit was decided without his connivance. Inheritances were cancelled – if Verres said the word. The properties of farmers were robbed of countless sums. Allies were treated as enemies; Roman citizens were tortured and put to death like slaves. Criminals of the deepest dye would bribe their way to acquittal, while men of impeccable honesty were prosecuted in their absence, and convicted and banished unheard ... It was an appalling disgrace for our country.

From Cicero, *Against Verres*, 70 BC

Race and religion also affected the application of the law. Foreigners were treated in the same way as the lower classes, and were clearly regarded as inferior. Under the emperors religion became a test of loyalty, and subject peoples were allowed to retain their own gods only if they also worshipped the emperor. Christians refused to do so and were persecuted. Sources **I**, **J** and **K** describe the Romans' attitude to religion.

Source I Religion in the Empire

What keeps the Empire united is religion. It is cloaked in so much pomp and plays such a large part in private and public affairs, that nothing can fight its influence.

Written by Polybius, a Greek historian of Rome, in the second century AD

Source J Why Christians were persecuted

The Christians were a special case ... The occasional outbursts of persecution against other contemporary religions can usually be explained on the grounds of politics, or concern with morals or public order; but Christians and Jews were different, because they refused to take part in the civic religion. Jews were given special licence and sanction by the Romans as a national characteristic. Yet Christians were persecuted for being Christians.

From J.A. Crook, *Law and Life of Rome*, 1967

Source K Mosaic illustrating the kind of punishment endured by Christians

Questions

1 How do Sources **I** and **J** explain the treatment of Christians shown in Source **K**?

2 In the context of your wider knowledge, do these sources suggest that the treatment of Christians was typical of Roman attitudes, or were they a special case?

3 Using all the sources and your wider knowledge, explain how the relationship between law and justice was affected by:
  • wealth and status;
  • the influence of attitudes and beliefs;
  • the effectiveness of law enforcement.

Race and justice in Roman Britain

▶ **How did the Romans treat the subject peoples of their empire?**

Boudicca's revolt

The Roman conquest of Britain began in AD 43, and by AD 47 the southern part had been conquered. According to their normal pattern the Romans left a number of client kings and allies in control of their own lands, but they also established colonies of soldiers and ex-soldiers in certain areas, in order to have reliable citizens at key points. One of these was the settlement at Camulodunum (Colchester) in the kingdom of the Iceni.

Prasutagus, king of the Iceni, died in AD 60, leaving his kingdom jointly to the emperor and his own family. He hoped that this would maintain the partnership that he had enjoyed with the Romans, and protect his kingdom, people and family. Instead his lands were seized and his family was maltreated by the Romans. His wife, Boudicca, led a revolt of the Iceni and other local tribes. While the governor of Britain, Suetonius Paulinus, was occupied in the west, Camulodunum, Londinium (London) and Verulamium (St Albans) were sacked and their Roman inhabitants massacred. Boudicca's army was eventually defeated on the battlefield by Suetonius, and she took poison. Sources **A** to **F** describe the rebellion in more detail.

Source A Tacitus on the causes of the revolt

Prasutagus, king of the Iceni, had died and left the emperor as co-heir with his two daughters, hoping to preserve his kingdom from attack. But kingdom and household alike were plundered like prizes of war, the one by Roman officers, the other by Roman slaves. His widow, Boudicca, was flogged and their daughters raped. The Icenian chiefs were deproved of their hereditary estates and the king's own relatives were treated like slaves.

The humiliated Iceni rebelled and with them the Trinobantes and others. They particularly hated the Roman ex-soldiers at Camulodunum. The settlers drove the Trinobantes from their homes and lands, and called them prisoners and slaves. A temple was erected to the divine Claudius: this was a blatant stronghold of foreign rule, and its priests drained the wealth of the country by taxes.

From Tacitus, *Annals of Imperial Rome*, early second century AD

Source B The Britons' attitude to injustice

The Britons bear conscription, the tribute [tax] and their other obligations to the Empire without complaint, provided there is no injustice. That they take extremely ill; for they can bear to be ruled by others, but not to be their slaves.

From Tacitus, *Annals of Imperial Rome*, early second century AD

Source C Cassius Dio on the causes of the revolt

An excuse for the war was found in the seizing of money that Claudius had given to the foremost Britons; for the procurator said it was lent and had to be paid back. This was one reason for the uprising; another was ... that Seneca [a Roman senator and adviser to the emperor] had lent to the islanders forty million sesterces [that they did not want] at a good rate of interest, and then demanded its repayment all at once. But the person who was most important in rousing the natives and persuading them to fight the Romans was Buduica. This woman assembled her army, to the number of some 120,000 ... and then led them against the Romans. This enabled her to sack and plunder two Roman cities and to wreak indescribable slaughter.

From Cassius Dio, *Roman History*, early third century AD

◆**Q**uestions

1 Who does Tacitus blame for Boudicca's rebellion (Sources **A** and **B**)? Tacitus was writing shortly after the rebellion. Is his evidence likely to be reliable?

2 Would the actions of the Romans in Britain be considered crimes in Roman law (Sources **A** and **C**)?

3 What new information does Cassius Dio provide about the causes of the revolt (Source **D**)? Who does he blame, and how does his account differ from that given by Tacitus?

Source D   The defeat of Boudicca

Because Suetonius was outnumbered, he decided to sacrifice Londinium to save the province as a whole. Those inhabitants who stayed, because they were women, old, or attached to the place, were slaughtered by the enemy. For the British did not take or sell prisoners. They could not wait to cut throats, hang, burn and crucify. Verulamium suffered the same fate.

   Suetonius collected the Fourteenth Legion and detachments of the Twentieth, together with the nearest available auxiliaries – amounting to nearly ten thousand armed men – and decided to attack without further delay … He had a glorious victory; according to one report almost eighty thousand Britons fell. The Britons had brought their wives with them to see their victory, and fled with difficulty since their ring of wagons blocked the outlets. The Romans did not spare even the women.

From Tacitus, *Annals of Imperial Rome*, early second century AD

Source E   A nineteenth-century artist's impression of Boudicca

Source F   The sack of London

Archaeological evidence makes the catastrophe that enveloped London in AD 60 dramatically clear. Wherever you dig into the foundations of London you come across a red and black layer of burned ash and soot … There is a horde of money whose owner buried it for safety, but never came back to collect it …
   [Claims about casualties and atrocities] may be an exaggeration, but there is no doubt that many settlers met with cruel deaths. The later writer, Cassius Dio, may just be adding lurid detail to titillate his readers when he describes how rich Roman women were hung up, their breasts cut off and sown to their mouths, how they were tortured and impaled on sharpened stakes – but it may be, as Tacitus implies, that such rites were done in fulfilment of religious practices demanded by the druids.

From M. Wood, *In Search of the Dark Ages*, 1981

The Romans' attitude to the conquered

Boudicca's revolt seems to show that the Romans treated subject peoples unfairly. However, to examine this issue more carefully, consider Sources **G** to **L**, which give further details of life in Britain under Roman rule, in peace as well as in war.

Source G   Tacitus describes the conquest of Mona (Anglesey), a Druidic centre and sacred place

The enemy lined the shore in a dense armed mass … Close by stood Druids, raising their hands to heaven and screaming dreadful curses … The Roman soldiers urged each other on, not to fear the horde … and they bore down on their opponents, enveloping them in the flames of their own torches. Suetonius garrisoned the conquered island. The groves devoted to Mona's barbarous superstitions he demolished. For it was their religion to drench their altars in the blood of prisoners and consult their gods by means of human entrails.

From Tacitus, *Annals of Imperial Rome*, early second century AD

And Jupiter declared, 'I set upon the Romans bounds neither of space nor of time: I have bestowed upon them Empire without limit' … Forget not, Roman, that it is your special genius to rule nations; to impose the ways of peace, to spare the defeated, and to crush those proud men who will not submit.

From Virgil, *Aeneid*, late first century BC

Source H   The Roman mission, according to the poet Virgil

Source I   Roman villas and towns

The Roman conquest of Britain resulted in a large number of changes ... The most obvious were the development of villas and the foundation of towns. The cities were central to the Roman political system, as they represented the centres of government and administration ... Although Roman Britain of the fourth century was very different from the island of 100 BC, the structural changes took place gradually in the later Roman period, rather than suddenly at the time of the Roman invasion.

From M. Millett, 'Settlement and Society', in *The Cambridge Historical Encyclopaedia of Great Britain and Ireland*

Source J
Reconstruction of the Roman villa at Lullingstone, Kent

Source K   Map showing the distribution of villas, towns and roads in Roman Britain

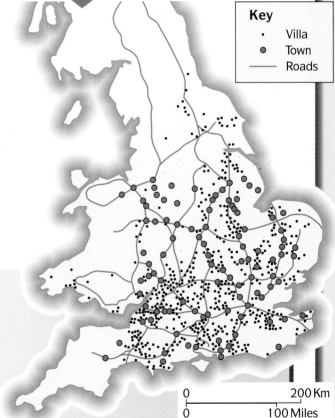

Key

· Villa
● Town
— Roads

0 ——————— 200 Km
0 ——————— 100 Miles

Another major benefit of Roman rule was the establishment of an adequate system of law and order. In most provinces, native laws, where they existed, were still respected, but the Roman system of administration provided proper courts where disputes could be settled.

From J. Wacher, *The Coming of Rome*, 1979

Source L   The rule of law in Britain

Questions

1 What impression is given of the British by the Roman writers in Sources **D** and **F**? How far was this justified?

2 Using the evidence in Sources **A** to **F** and your own knowledge, write a short account of Boudicca's revolt. In it, you should explain:
   • why the revolt broke out; • who was responsible for this; • the behaviour of the rebels; • how the revolt was suppressed.

3 Look at Source **G**. Who were the Druids? What did the Romans think of them?

4 What does Source **H** suggest about Roman attitudes to other races? How does this help you understand Roman treatment of other people?

5 Look at Sources **I** to **L**. How did the British change as a result of the Roman conquest?

6 'The Romans respected the British, so long as they behaved like Romans.' How far do you agree with this statement? Base your answer on your own knowledge and on the sources you have studied.

7 To what extent does the evidence in these sources allow you to make judgements about the way in which the Romans treated the subject peoples in their Empire?

3 The development of the English legal system

The invasions of Britain

▶ **What changes took place after the Romans left Britain?**

The Dark Ages

In the fifth century AD, the Roman Empire in the West collapsed due to internal disunity and barbarian invasions by the Goths, Vandals and Franks. The north German tribes – Angles, Saxons and Jutes – invaded Britain. As a result many people fled from the towns into the countryside, and the Roman roads, buildings and libraries fell into disrepair. The invaders were mainly farmers looking for new land, and having driven out the British, they settled in villages. This period is known as the Dark Ages, because to people of the time it represented the end of civilisation, and because later generations know so little about it. The invasions and their results are described in Source **A**.

New kingdoms emerged, but they were quite different to Roman Britain. They were small and relatively poor, relied on subsistence farming and were often threatened by attack. The invaders brought their own traditions and laws, based on family links, blood feuds and loyalty to tribal lords. In many ways they were sensible arrangements for rural settlements, and similar systems gradually developed in the west of England and Wales. The new kingdoms also developed law enforcement systems of their own.

Anglo-Saxon England

The influence of the Church, the emergence of early towns around monastic and strategic centres, and increasing literacy improved the social and government structure of England. Despite Viking invasions and continual wars, tenth-century England was a prosperous peasant society, governed by a Christian monarchy and nobility, with power based on personal loyalties and services paid in return for land. The country was divided into *shires* and *hundreds* (a group of villages) which were governed by royal officials known as *ealdormen* and *reeves*, and which ensured that the scattered settlements and villages were brought together at regular intervals.

Depopulation in the fifth and sixth centuries was indeed drastic. Many people fled westwards, or else to Brittany, and epidemic disease may have played its part. Why was Roman Britain obliterated so much more completely than Roman Gaul? One reason is that the settlers were different; another may be that the Britons themselves had changed greatly between the early fifth and mid-sixth centuries. The earliest Welsh poems show a society remarkably like that of the Saxons, dominated by the same loyalties and with the same emphasis on treasure, gift-giving and the fellowship of warriors in their chieftain's hall. Even if no Saxon had ever set foot in Britain, it may be that its Roman civilisation would have proved too fragile to last.

From J. Blair, 'The Anglo-Saxon Period', in *The Oxford Illustrated History of Great Britain*, 1993

Source A Britain after the Romans

Source B Timeline of the main events in the development of Anglo-Saxon England

450–500	Arrival of earliest settlers in Kent and on south coast of England
500–600	Formation of early kingdoms
560–660	Spread of Christianity; Synod of Whitby (AD 664) establishes the authority of the Church of Rome throughout England
757–96	King Offa of Mercia claims overlordship as 'King of the English'
789	First record of Viking raids; followed by attacks on monasteries in 793 (Lindisfarne), 794 (Jarrow) and 795 (Iona)
865–870	Danish conquest of eastern England
871–899	Reign of King Alfred in Wessex; Danish invasion halted and England divided into kingdom of Wessex (Saxon) and the Danelaw
899–954	Reconquest of the Danelaw by Alfred's successors, Edward (899–924), Athelstan (924–39) and Edmund (939–46)
959–76	Reign of King Edgar; rebuilding of the Church and monastic life
979–1016	Reign of Ethelred the Unready; new Viking invasions lead to conquest of England by Danish king, Swein; Swein is accepted as king by the English nobility, and is followed by his son Cnut
1042	After Cnut's death, the throne passes to Edward the Confessor, son of Ethelred, who had grown up in exile in Normandy

The Norman Conquest

In 1066 England was again invaded and conquered, this time by William of Normandy. William granted land to his followers, but did not displace the inhabitants except where they resisted, for example in the 'harrying of the north' in 1069–70. The Saxon nobility who led rebellions were destroyed, and a new ruling class and culture was imposed, but the structure of government, the Church and the system of land-holding, illustrated in Source **C**, was taken over largely as it stood.

Source C   The feudal system in medieval England

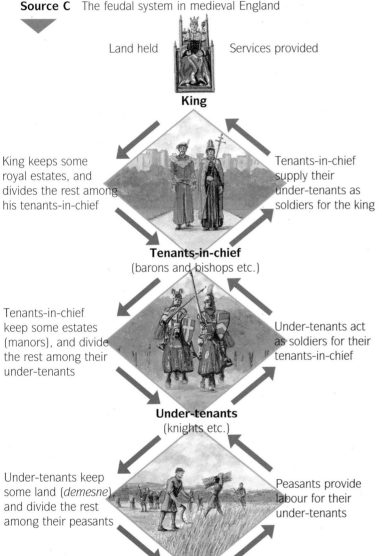

Land held   Services provided

King

King keeps some royal estates, and divides the rest among his tenants-in-chief

Tenants-in-chief supply their under-tenants as soldiers for the king

Tenants-in-chief
(barons and bishops etc.)

Tenants-in-chief keep some estates (manors), and divide the rest among their under-tenants

Under-tenants act as soldiers for their tenants-in-chief

Under-tenants
(knights etc.)

Under-tenants keep some land (*demesne*) and divide the rest among their peasants

Peasants provide labour for their under-tenants

Peasants

So there is a great deal of *continuity* between Saxon and Norman England. The Normans brought new influences and ideas, but they did not destroy the existing society. The English were a conquered race, and occasionally this resentment led to popular protest or sympathy for rebels and outlaws, but over time, social and cultural differences softened. When problems arose, they tended to come from within the ruling class, jostling for greater power or undermining weak kings. In theory, medieval England was a settled, law-abiding society. The reality, however, could be very different.

Source D   Timeline of the Norman kings and their troubles

1066–87	William I; faces constant rebellion from Saxon nobility and also French attacks in Normandy
1087–1100	William Rufus
1100–35	Henry I
1135–54	Stephen, nephew of Henry I; faces civil war because of claim to the throne by Matilda, Henry's daughter
1154–89	Henry II; successful ruler, but faces rebellions by three sons and quarrel with the Church
1189–99	Richard I, 'the Lionheart'; faces rebellion by barons while absent fighting Crusades
1199–1216	King John; quarrels with Church and barons; forced to sign Magna Carta
1216–72	Henry III; England is ruled by barons while Henry is a child; barons later rebel under Simon de Montfort
1272–1307	Edward I; strong king, conquers Wales and invades Scotland
1307–27	Edward II; fails against Scots, is deposed by barons and murdered
1327–77	Edward III; successful in wars against France, but dies leaving baby grandson Richard as king
1377–99	Richard II; faces Peasants' Revolt and barons' rebellion; is deposed and murdered in 1399, leading eventually to civil war, the Wars of the Roses (1451–85)

Questions

1 What races made up the medieval 'English'?

2 Why might Roman law have less influence on the laws of England than in other parts of Europe?

Anglo-Saxon law

 How did the early English legal system work?

From blood-feud to wergild

The foundations of the English legal system were laid by the Anglo-Saxons. Among these settlers, punishment of criminals was first left to the victim or his family – a form of personal revenge. This led to a system of blood feuds, highlighting the importance of family (*kin*) and lordship in early Anglo-Saxon society. A free man would be supported by his kin; a slave or serf would be punished or defended by his lord. But there were problems with such a system on a large national scale and so kings issued laws, or *dooms* (as in Source **A**). Gradually a system of payment was introduced known as *wergild* (see Source **B**), which was payable to the victim's family, and *bot gild*, which was payable to an injured party.

Source A Dooms of Alfred: from the legal code issued by King Alfred in 871

I King Alfred have collected these dooms and ordered to be written down ... those which our predecessors observed and which were also pleasing to me. And those which were not pleasing to me, by the advice of my witan [council of advisers] I have rejected, ordering them to be observed only as amended. I have not ventured to put in writing much of my own, being uncertain what might please those who shall come after us ... I, then, Alfred, king of the West Saxons, have shown these dooms to all my witan, who have declared it is the will of all that they be observed ...

 **Source B** Wergild and the structure of Anglo-Saxon society

KING
Wergild: 8200 silver shillings

NOBLE
Wergild: 600–1200 silver shillings
A noble usually owned several estates. This land was often given by the king in return for service in times of war. Sometimes the noble sat on the witan, or king's council. He was in charge of collecting the king's taxation and military services on his estates. He made sure that the king's law was carried out.

CHURL OR FREE PEASANT
Wergild: 200 silver shillings
The churl, or free peasant, could own, sell, buy or pass on land to children. He often rented land from the lord in return for money, goods, or services. He paid taxes and did military service. Peasants formed the largest section of the population. Although free, they were often very poor.

SLAVES
No wergild
A slave could be bought or sold. A person could be born a slave or become a slave because he broke the law or was captured in war. A freeman could sell himself into slavery if his crops failed or he was in debt. When Christianity spread throughout Britain, many slaves were freed because the Church was against slavery.

The new system rested on three institutions – lordship, justice of the monarchy and the village community.

Lordship

The basis of Anglo-Saxon society was land, and land was not owned, but held from a lord. This was true both for freemen and for serfs, but a difference lay in the kind of personal services that each owed. Land was granted in a ceremony in which the tenant did *homage* and swore loyalty to his lord, so becoming the lord's *vassal*. The relationship carried rights and duties on both sides, and it was this which made lordship the basis of law (see Source **C**). A man who had no lord stood outside society, as described in Source **D**. For much of the medieval period, over 80 per cent of crime was dealt with in the village court before the lord or his steward.

Source C   The relationship of lord and vassal

The relationship of lord and vassal was the key to much law ... One of the principal duties of a lord was to uphold the rights of his vassals. First the vassals' rights on his land had to be protected. Secondly, where a lord's vassals were in conflict with one another, he had to make judgements between them. The lord needed a court and one of the principal elements in lordship was the right (even the duty) to hold a court. In that court, vassals got justice, and the lord got honour, power and profit.

From J. Briggs et al., *Crime and Punishment in England*, 1996

Source D   The Declaration of King Athelstan (924–39)

With regard to lordless men, from whom no [legal] satisfaction can be obtained, we have declared that their relatives shall be commanded to settle them in a fixed residence where they shall become amenable to public law, and find them a lord at a public meeting. If, however, on the appointed day they will not or cannot, he shall be henceforth an outlaw [outside the protection of the law] and he who encounters him may assume him to be a thief and kill him.

Justice

The king had no lord but God and his power was supreme. The nobility held land from the king, and were therefore his vassals; he too, therefore, needed a court. Also, groups such as women, the clergy and foreign residents had no lord, and therefore had to be protected by the king. A system of royal courts had to be established to enforce law in the kingdom as a whole.

By the year 1000 there was a system of shire and hundred courts covering the whole kingdom. The hundred courts met every four weeks and all freemen attended. They dealt with minor crime, but the more serious cases would be taken to the shire court, which met approximately twice a year. This court covered an area equivalent to a modern county, and was run by the *shire-reeve* (the origin of 'sheriff') who was chosen by the king. The king sent him written instructions, known as writs. The shire court was attended by representatives from the hundreds, with the local nobility and senior clergy, who often acted as judges. There were also special courts in the boroughs, which were towns holding a royal charter.

Community

As people lived in small settlements, they worked together and depended on one another. They developed a system of collective responsibility enforced by the *tithing* and *borh*. A tithing was a group of men, originally ten but later varying in size, who were collectively responsible for the behaviour of each member. If a man committed a crime his tithing had to bring him to court, or pay compensation to the victim. In addition, any man accused of a crime had to pay a sum of money, known as borh, to the head of his tithing, to ensure his appearance in court. This worked like the modern system of paying bail. The whole system added community pressure to the lord's power, to help prevent crime and ensure punishment if crimes were committed.

Questions

1   How did blood feuds involve family, lordship and the community?

2   How and why did these relationships form the basis of the Anglo-Saxon legal system?

Enforcing Anglo-Saxon law

▶ **What were Anglo-Saxon trials and punishments?**
Did the Norman Conquest change the system?

The law suit in action

Although King Alfred and most of his successors issued law codes, Anglo-Saxon law was never codified in full before the Norman Conquest in 1066. Much law had been handed down orally (i.e. without being written down) but no effort had been made codify it until the days of the Norman law writers.

The procedure in law suits was strict and formal: the plaintiff summoned the defendant to appear in the *moot* ('meeting'). If he did not appear he automatically lost the case. If he, or his family, did not then pay the compensations involved he became an outlaw. If he appeared, the plaintiff had to swear that his motives were honest, and then the defendant was allowed to swear that he was innocent. He then used 'compurgators' to support his claim of innocence. These were not witnesses to prove the facts, but were really character witnesses: the value of their statements depended on their status in society. If the defendant came to court and performed the oath in full, the suit was ended and he was clear. The law worked on a principle that denial of guilt was stronger than accusation.

The ordeals

If, however, the defendant was of suspicious character who had been frequently accused, or if he had ever been convicted of perjury (lying when under oath), he was no longer 'oath-worthy'. Then the plaintiff could produce compurgators and make an oath. The defendant could respond by going to 'ordeal' – the judgement of God. The Church then took control. After a three-day fast and prayers the defendant was given the chance to confess his guilt. He was then given a choice between the ordeals of iron and water. If the defendant was a woman, hot water or iron was usually chosen.

After these ordeals the wound would be bound up, then examined after three days. If it was healing cleanly the defendant was innocent. If a man was convicted he was condemned by the court to the punishment prescribed in the laws. The most common punishment was the payment of compensation and fines (see Source **A**). Some crimes, however, were considered to be 'bootless', and not open to compensation. In these cases – arson, house-breaking, open theft, obvious murder, and treachery to one's lord – the punishment was death and loss of property.

The ordeal of cold water

The ordeals

Ordeal of cold water. The man was tied in a crouching position, and suspended on a rope. He was then thrown into water, and if he sank to a certain depth, was regarded as innocent. If, however, the pure water rejected him – that is, he floated – he was considered to be guilty.

Ordeal of hot water. The defendant had to pick a stone out of a cauldron of boiling water. For a minor crime, it required only the hand to be submerged, but in more serious crimes, the cauldron was deep enough to require the arm to enter the water as far as the elbow.

Ordeal of iron. The defendant had to carry a red-hot iron bar for a certain distance. The distance and the weight of the bar were varied according to the seriousness of the crime.

Source A From the legal code of Alfred the Great

▼

Every man's oath should be true and his promises kept ... If a man breaks his pledges or oaths, he must spend forty days in prison. If a man says false things in public against another, he is to have his tongue cut out or pay a fine in proportion to his wergild. If anyone plots against the king's life, or shelters the king's enemies, he is liable to lose his life and all that he owns. If any man steals in church his hand is to be cut off, or he may pay a fine in proportion to his blood money or wergild.

The Normans and the English legal system

Norman law was based on *mund* – an area of peace and order around every man's home. As the king's *mund* covered the whole kingdom, he was ultimately responsible for all his subjects, and could claim authority in matters of crime affecting the peace of his kingdom. In practice his vassals exercised authority within their lands and estates, but it was always clear that they did so by his permission.

The Normans found that the English legal system could operate within their ideas, and so did not attempt to replace the system. William granted land to his Normans in return for personal homage and military service, and the English became the vassals of these Norman lords. Most peasants were *villeins* – unfree tenants owing personal service to their lord – and their lords held manorial courts to dispense justice. Outside these courts, the king's *mund* could be exercised in the shire and hundred courts.

The king introduced special forest laws covering whole areas of countryside, and totalling about one third of the country. The forests were not just woodlands but included farms and settlements, as well as the wilder, more remote parts of the country, often used by outlaws. Forest laws were intended to keep order in these difficult areas.

As Source **B** shows, there was a great deal of continuity between the Saxon and Norman systems of law. Sources **C** and **D** illustrate this continuity in the reigns of William and his successors.

Source B The Anglo-Saxon legal system and its Norman equivalent

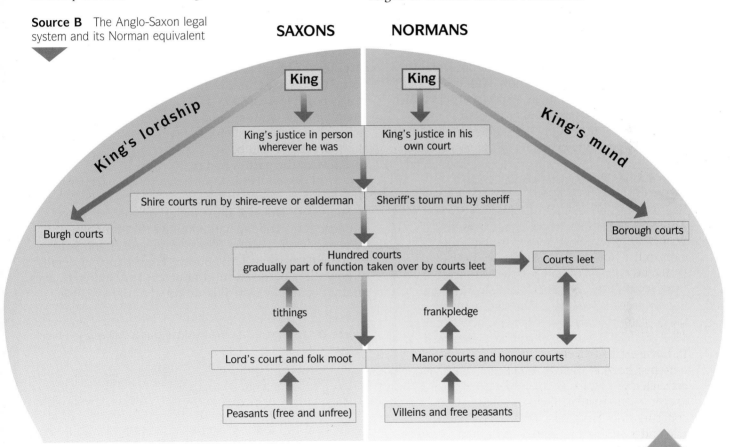

Source C
A proclamation issued by William I, re-issued in the reign of Henry I (1100–35)

This also I command and will, that all shall have and keep the law of King Edward [the Confessor] … together with those additions which I have established for the benefit of the English people.

Know that I grant and order that henceforth my shire courts and hundred courts shall meet in the same places and at the same terms as they were accustomed to do in the time of King Edward, and not otherwise.

Source D
From orders sent by Henry I in 1100 to the leading men of Worcestershire

Questions

1 What kinds of crime seem to have occurred in Anglo-Saxon England?

2 How was guilt or innocence decided?

3 What punishments were used?

4 What do these methods tell us about Anglo-Saxon society and attitudes? Why was the same system adopted by the Normans?

Enforcing Norman law

▶ *How did the Normans punish crimes?*

Developments under the Normans

The Normans did introduce some changes to the legal system. They changed the language of the law, using French as the language of the courts, and Latin for keeping records. Some new arrangements had to be made for cases which involved both English and Frenchmen, where Norman and English law could not operate separately. Source **A** shows how William defined the murder of a Norman as a special crime, which suggests there was continuing English resentment. Source **B** provides an example of how he tried to combine elements of the two systems.

Source A A declaration of William I in 1070

▼

I will that all the men whom I have brought with me, or who have come after me [from Normandy] shall be protected by my peace [*mund*] and shall live in quiet. And if one of them is killed, his murderer's lord shall capture the slayer within five days if he can; but if not, he shall start to pay to me forty-six marks of silver so long as his possessions last. But when they are exhausted, the whole hundred in which the slaying occurred shall pay in common what remains.

Source B From the summary of William I's laws, published and confirmed by Henry I

▼

It was also decreed that if a Frenchman accuses an Englishman of perjury or murder, theft or homicide, the Englishman may defend himself as he prefers, either through the ordeal of hot water or through trial by battle ... If an Englishman accuses a Frenchman, and is unwilling to prove his charge by ordeal or trial by battle, I will, nevertheless, that the Frenchman purge himself [show his innocence] by a strong oath.

Trial by battle

The reference in Source **B** to trial by battle points to a new element introduced by the Normans. Both parties in a dispute were expected to fight until one died or yielded. In disputes over land (or if one party was disabled, or a woman) it was possible to use a 'champion' to fight on your behalf, but if crimes such as theft or murder had been committed, the parties had to appear in person. If the loser survived the battle, they were hanged.

Sources **C**, **D** and **E** illustrate an example of what happened in a trial by battle, telling the story of a combat between Walter Bloweberme and Hamo Stare which took place in 1249. Source **F** gives further details of how these battles were conducted, and Source **G** gives another contemporary illustration of a trial by battle.

Source D Background to the battle between Walter and Hamo

▼

Walter Bloweberme accuses Hamo Stare that they were at the house of Edeline Cross at Winchester, and there stole clothes and other goods. Hamo had as his share two coats. Walter offers to prove by his body that Hamo was guilty. Hamo comes and denies everything and says that he is willing to defend himself by his body. So it is decided that there be battle between. The battle takes place and Hamo has given in.

From the Hampshire Court Records, 1249

Source E Bill for the purchase of equipment for the battle between Walter and Hamo

▼

Purchase of:		
	2 shields	*13s 4d*
	2 wooden staves	*3s*
	white leather, felt, and	
	linen cloth for tunics	*8s 3d*

Source F How the trial by battle was conducted

In the thirteenth century, a lawyer said that the loss of the molar teeth did not enable a person to claim exemption from the trial by battle, but the absence of incisors did. The combatants had to take oaths that sorcery would not be used. The accused had to plead 'not guilty' and throw down a glove, declaring that he would defend it with his body. The accuser picked it up and declared that he would make good the charge, 'body for body'. If they broke their weapons, they had to fight on with hands, fists, nails, teeth, feet and legs until one called out 'craven' which was a confession of guilt. The loser was executed.

From R. Whiting, *Crime and Punishment*, 1986

Trial by battle was relatively rare but it survived longer than ordeal, which was formally abolished in England in 1219. Wyville, Bishop of Salisbury, who died in 1375, had a funeral brass which showed the champion who fought for him, and won, in a dispute over possession of Sherborne Castle.

Source G Trial by battle

Questions

1 What new laws did the Normans introduce?

2 Why were these laws necessary?

3 Use your knowledge of the period to explain why the Normans believed that trial by battle was fair.

4 The evolution of English law

Henry II and the restoration of the legal system

 How did English common law develop?

For a long time from 1066 English and Norman law existed side by side, but in the mid-eleventh century, during the reign of King Stephen, a civil war led to a breakdown of law and order. His successor, Henry II, needed to restore the legal system and drew together the common practice of English and Norman law. This became the basis of English common law – a mixture of written laws, customs and practice which has built up since then. In 1164 he issued the Constitutions of Clarendon, which summarised the existing law and procedures, followed by later additions known as *assizes*. The most important of these were the Assizes of Clarendon in 1166 and the Assizes of Northampton in 1176. This unit examines the main features of the legal system he restored.

Law courts and judges

The shire and hundred courts remained important but were now supervised by central courts and judges who were sent on *eyre* or circuit (see Source **A**). England was divided into six circuits and judges were to visit each place twice yearly. They were given four main duties:

- *general eyre*: to visit and check on crime and policing;
- *oyer and terminer* [to hear and give judgement]: to deal with serious crimes;
- *trailbaston*: to deal with violent crimes;
- *gaol delivery*: twice yearly, to try those held in gaol.

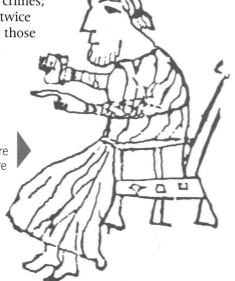

Source A
A medieval picture of a justice in eyre

The name assizes was then transferred to the shire court sessions that the judges attended. These dealt with criminal law but people also brought civil cases to them, and in 1178 the king set up the Court of Common Pleas in Westminster to deal with civil cases. Soon afterwards a similar court was added to deal with criminal cases, called the Court of the King's Bench.

Law enforcement

The *sheriff* was responsible for law and order in a shire. Writs (legal instructions) were now written to a standard form, and had to be returned, to show that they had been carried out. They were supervised by the officials of the Exchequer, a financial court set up by Henry I, and by the Justiciar. The Justiciar could make legal decisions and people could appeal to him, just as they would to the king. The courts of Exchequer, Common Pleas and King's Bench provided a permanent legal authority for all free subjects to seek justice in.

The system by which people were charged and brought to court was also improved. A case could still be started by a plaintiff, or by the use of informers, or 'approvers', who offered evidence against others in return for a lighter sentence themselves. The local community were also encouraged to bring people to trial, by acting as a 'jury of presentment', or *grand jury*. In these cases the accused was kept in gaol until gaol delivery, when the case would be heard by a judge on eyre. Each shire had to provide a gaol and gaolers who would be paid by the accused to keep them in reasonable comfort. Some gaolers abused this system and it often led to appalling conditions in many gaols.

Trial by jury

Using juries involved the community in peace-keeping. Gradually this concept was extended through the use of *petty juries* to decide on issues of guilt or innocence. There were disadvantages to trial by battle and ordeal, and compurgation could easily be corrupted. But juries were initially only available at the assizes, and even this system was not perfect.

For example, juries could be bribed or intimidated, and corrupt sheriffs could easily choose a jury to help or damage particular parties. However, it was still a more reliable method of trial than any other, and gradually it improved (see Source **B**). During the thirteenth century greater attention was paid to rules of evidence, and jury trial became normal practice (as implied by Source **C**). In the fourteenth century it was agreed that no one should serve on the jury if the accused objected to them, and that verdicts had to be unanimous.

Source B   The early days of trial by jury

At first, trial by jury was not considered as trustworthy as the God-controlled ordeal procedure. Juries were reluctant to convict neighbours of a felony [serious crime], as that meant a death sentence. Those who were most likely to be found guilty were those caught in the act, or with stolen goods on them, and notorious characters and strangers. Gradually, courts made more of an effort to obtain evidence.

From R. Whiting, *Crime and Punishment*, 1986

Source C   The punishment of *peine fort et dure* ('strong and severe punishment')

From 1275 by the first Statute of Westminster, notoriously bad people who refused a jury trial were faced with peine fort et dure ... This meant being imprisoned with weights placed on the chest while lying flat on the ground, or sometimes with a sharp stone underneath the body to break the criminal's back, until he agreed to a trial. Some men would deliberately endure the agony until death, in order to avoid the confiscation of their property which went with being found guilty of a felony.

From R. Whiting, *Crime and Punishment*, 1986

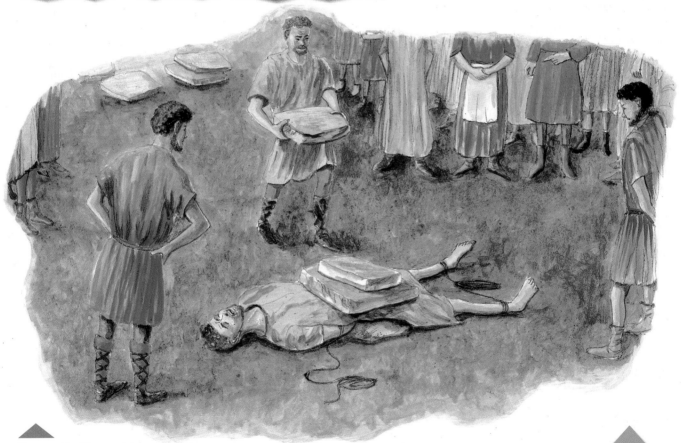

Source D   The punishment *peine fort et dure* in action

Questions

How was the legal system established by Henry II improved by:
a) written laws; **b)** judges on circuit; **c)** standard writs; **d)** juries?

Later developments

▶ *How did the law develop in later medieval England?*

New laws

Many of the key elements of modern law derive directly from the system established by Henry II. Custom and past practice remained important, but the assizes allowed laws to be updated and royal charters such as the Magna Carta of 1215 also added to the body of law. Like Roman law, English common law was able to change and develop in the light of experience.

Under Richard I a new official – the *coroner* – dealt with suspicious deaths. The coroner in each shire could appoint a jury to investigate a death and decide if a crime had been committed. If so, they reported the crime and any suspects to the sheriff, who would then arrest and imprison the suspect until the next eyre. In 1285 Edward I introduced a new law requiring men to serve in the sheriff's *posse comitatus* ('force of the county'), to chase and catch criminals. The hundred was also now required to provide men and weapons, to keep the woods cut back from roads to prevent ambush, and to pay a fine if they failed to catch the criminal. This was a development of the old system of hue and cry when tithings were called out to the chase. Again it emphasised the use of the community in dealing with crime.

The justice of the peace

The most important of all developments was the introduction of the *justice of the peace* (JP) . This had its origins under Richard I when some knights were appointed Keepers of the Peace in unruly areas, and in 1314 they were given the power to arrest people. In 1361, now known as justices of the peace, they were given the power to 'bind over' unruly people to keep the peace. By 1439 there were about twenty in each county, who met four times a year in *quarter sessions*, to hear criminal cases and deal with local issues. Soon these sessions took over the business of the hundred courts, and in 1461 the justices of the peace were given responsibility for the shire courts in place of the sheriff.

Lord's and manorial courts

Although royal courts were important, for most of the population justice was sought in the local court, which was held by the lord or his representative, the reeve or steward. *Honour courts* covered all the villages and manors under a lord, while *manor courts* covered one manor only. Some lords had extra rights, such as 'view of frankpledge' which gave them similar powers to those of the sheriff over the tithings in the hundred courts. Later, *courts leet* were developed. In these, juries made up of the heads of tithings were summoned to deal with local crime in a court with the lord acting as judge. Source **A** describes the sort of crimes that were dealt with in them, while Sources **B** and **C** give examples of these crimes and punishments taken from the court rolls, or records.

Source A The court leet

> The court leet, like the manor court, acted for the community as much as for the lord, and free men and bondmen sat together on the juries ... The court's staple diet consisted of presentments of assaults ranging from blood-shedding to 'villain words'; of the obstruction of highways and water-courses; of breaches of Henry III's assizes forbidding the harbouring of strangers and fixing the price of ale; and of the raising of the hue and cry.
>
> From A. Harding, *England in the Thirteenth Century*, 1993

Source B From the court rolls of the manor of Brambelshute, Hampshire, 8 February 1333

> Mercy [fine] 2½p – Robert atte Downe amerced [fined] for 15 sheep in the lord's wood; by surety of William le Voghel
> Mercy 2p – Robert atte Lee amerced for 30 sheep in the same place; by surety of William le Voghel
> Mercy ½p – Robert le Dow puts himself in mercy [fined] for unjustly impounding the horse of Henry Gasse
> Mercy 1p – Peter atte Valghe amerced because he failed to perform autumn services as he owed
> Mercy 2½p – Robert atte Downe amerced for a trespass against the lord at the mill
> Mercy 1p – Robert Faber amerced for defaming William Cissor by falsely accusing him of theft

Agnes, the wife of Thomas Reynald, is a nuisance and a thief. Fined 22p, later reduced. (1294)
Alice Oxhird has slept unlawfully with a man. Leywrite fine 2p. (1365)
Alice of Bellasis brews ale, but it is bad. Fine 10p. (1366)
Margaret Ster of Wolviston is fined 2p because she has slandered the ale taster. (1373)
Alice Tewer for sleeping unlawfully with a man. The tenth time she is accused of this. Fine 2p. (1400)
The wife of John Ireland is a gossip and a nuisance to her neighbours. She is ordered to get on better with her neighbours, or else she will not only pay a fine of 33p but have to get out of the village. (1465)
Katherine Sharp of Stockton is fined 16p for assaulting Elizabeth, the servant of Robert Burdon, at which [she drew] blood. She is fined another 10p for shedding the blood of John Joyfull. (1475)

Stocks in every town were used to humiliate petty criminals and hold those awaiting trial. (For the stocks and other punishments see Sources **D** to **F**.)

Some crimes, however, went beyond the powers of the manorial courts. Lords could execute thieves caught on their land with stolen goods, but crimes like homicide, robbery and rape had to be reported to the higher courts and coroners, and later to the judges on eyre.

Source D The stocks and other punishments

For the punishment of lesser crimes there were the stocks, the pillory and the ducking-stool. The pillory held the culprit by the neck and wrists ... and was a more painful punishment than the stocks. Occasionally the culprits' ears were nailed to the wooden board so that he could not hang his head when the spectators of his misery threw stones and rubbish at him; and sometimes his feet did not reach the platform, and he was throttled ... Prison was rarely used as a punishment, but debtors were kept in prison as were those awaiting trial. This could also prove a sentence of death, for those who could not pay the gaoler what he demanded were kept in appalling conditions.

From C. Hibbert, *The English*, 1994

Source E Deterrence and retribution

There were two aims behind punishments – deterrence [making people frightened to commit a similar crime] and retribution [making a criminal suffer for what he had done]. The Assize of Clarendon ruled that if one lost the ordeal, one would lose a foot and be given eight days to leave the country on pain of oulawry. The Assize of Northampton increased this to the loss of the right hand as well as a foot ... The Statute of Labourers in 1351 required stocks to be set up in all villages as 'open gaols' where runaway servants and labourers could be held until claimed by their masters. They were also used for drunkards, immorality, gamblers and vagrants [wandering unemployed].

From R. Whiting, *Crime and Punishmen*, 1986

Source F A medieval illustration of the stocks in use

Questions

1 What sorts of crime were dealt with by the local courts?

2 What forms of punishment were used? Which was used most often?

3 What do these sources reveal about medieval life and society?

4 How far do Sources **D** to **F** suggest that punishment was harsh?

5 Are they the same punishments as those applied in Sources **B** and **C**?

6 What reasons can you suggest for the conflicts and differences in the evidence?

5 Crime, society and religion

The influence of the Church

  ▶ **How did the Church use its legal powers?**

The Church and the Crown

As medieval society was deeply religious the Church had a great influence on everyday life. The role of the Church in England was further strengthened when William the Conqueror set up *church courts* for certain crimes, and to control the behaviour of priests. In the reign of Henry II the independence of the Church and the authority of the Pope led to quarrels about where power should lie. As a result of these quarrels, Thomas Becket, the Archbishop of Canterbury, was murdered by supporters of the King. After further quarrels between the Pope and King John, church privileges were confirmed in the Magna Carta. Only then was a more stable partnership between Church and king restored.

The Church and the legal system

The Church influenced the legal system in many different ways, and it was not always helpful. On the one hand it provided educated men to record laws, produce writs and act as judges, and encouraged more merciful punishments (see Source **A**). Criminals could also receive sanctuary in churches (see Source **B**).

Source A   From laws written for King Cnut by Archbishop Wulfstan in the eleventh century

> Christian men shall not be condemned to death for all too little; but one shall determine lenient punishments for the benefit of the people, and not destroy for a little matter God's own handiwork …

Source B   Seeking sanctuary

> Seeking sanctuary was one option for criminals. It gave them immunity from arrest for a week, and sometimes longer … after that they had to stand trial, or leave the kingdom. The aim was to give time for a settlement to be reached, emphasising the Christian idea of mercy. However, traitors, heretics, sorcerers, clerics and outlaws were denied sanctuary.
>
> Adapted from R. Whiting, *Crime and Punishment*, 1986

On the other hand, church courts could be lenient with those who pleaded 'benefit of clergy' so they had a more favourable trial (see Sources **C** and **D**), and the Church decided on some crimes because they challenged its power. For example, people with different religious beliefs could be found guilty of heresy and could be arrested and tortured (see Source **F**). Similarly, religious belief encouraged the persecution of minorities such as the Jews, and the belief that women were inferior, or even wicked (see Sources **G** and **H**).

Source C   Benefit of clergy

> The Church claimed the right to try all clergy in Church courts, a right known as 'benefit of clergy'. Since the Church courts could not impose the death sentence, this meant that those convicted of felonies (serious crimes) could get off lightly, as compared to the king's justice. There were probably about 40,000 ordained men in England, that is to say, one for every 25 or 30 adult people. In addition, there were thousands of men in minor orders – clerks, accountants, doctors, lawyers – who could qualify for benefit of clergy, through their education and training.
>
> From C. Hibbert, *The English*, 1994

Source D   Benefit of clergy

> There was doubt as to who could claim benefit of clergy. Anyone who had a monk's haircut was taken to be a cleric. So a man awaiting trial might have a quick haircut in gaol to deceive the authorities. By 1350 benefit extended to holders of Church posts, such as doorkeepers, and by the end of the 14th century to anyone who could read.
>
> Adapted from R. Whiting, *Crime and Punishment*, 1986

Source E Some monks abused their position, as this illustration of a monk with his mistress shows: both are in the stocks

Source F From an Act of 1401 entitled 'On the Burning of Heretics'. This was directed against the teachings of Wyclif and his followers, the Lollards

Many false persons do maliciously preach and teach these new doctrines against the holy Catholic Church; they make and write books, they wickedly instruct the people and stir them to rebellion ... From henceforth ... no one ... shall preach openly without a licence from a bishop; no one shall make, write or possess a book of such wicked doctrines. And if any persons be convicted of acting against this law, they shall be burnt before the people in a public place, so that their punishment shall strike fear into the hearts of others, so that no wicked doctrines may be tolerated.

Source G The Christian writer Gratian on female weakness, 1140

Adam was tempted by Eve, not she by him. It is right that he whom woman led into wrongdoing should have her under his direction, so that he may not fail a second time through female weakness.

Source H The story of Adam and Eve, as depicted in a painting from the twelfth century

Questions

1 What was the purpose of sanctuary (Source **B**)? Give three examples of either how it could help justice, or how it could hinder justice.

2 What is meant by 'benefit of clergy' in Sources **C** and **D**? How did this help or hinder justice?

3 What attitudes are being encouraged in Sources **F**, **G** and **H**?

4 How might these attitudes encourage injustice?

6 Law and the people in late medieval England

Justice and injustice

▶ *How far did the law provide justice for all people?*

Source A
The Magna Carta ▶

Rights and wrongs

In the thirteenth century the English legal system was based on customary and written law administered by feudal lords and royal officials. The Magna Carta, or Great Charter, was issued by King John in 1215 (see Source **A**). This established certain legal rights and principles for all free men, for example the right to be consulted about taxes and the right to a fair trial. And as the feudal system collapsed these rights began to apply to more and more people. From 1297 the modern parliament began to develop as representatives of the common people (Commons) met with the barons (Lords).

Justice, however, depends on good laws being fairly enforced, and as Source **B** shows, this did not always happen. This list of complaints suggests serious difficulties in enforcing the law. Problems arose from violence, intimidation and the corruption of officials. In addition, the lords and barons, whose task it was to uphold law and government, often abused their power for their own profit. These problems occurred mainly in times of political unrest, but they also seem to have lasted for long periods of time (see the table on p. 65).

Source B Anarchy in the thirteenth century

In the civil war between Henry III and Simon de Montfort [1254–60], marauding gangs of robbers overran the entire country. Commissioners appointed in 1305 found that these gangs had forcibly seized and held estates, bought others for paltry sums by threats, 'impeded and corrupted constables, bailiffs and the King's officers, invaded manor houses and plundered them from cellar to loft, attacked and maimed jurors and witnesses to prevent them telling the truth at assizes, and hired assassins for battery, assault and mayhem'.

Adapted from C. Hibbert, *The English*, 1994

This raises two main questions. How far did the law provide justice in medieval England and how did people react to injustice? Sources **C** to **F** will allow you to investigate and answer these questions.

Source C   Rights and duties in the villages

The village community's sense of its rights was upheld by the manor court, which belonged to the peasants as much as it did to the lord. In court, the first duty of the steward and reeve was to defend the lord's franchise, but the tenants themselves presented [reported] the customs of the manor and reported the customary levels of service.

From A. Harding, *England in the Thirteenth Century*, 1993

Source D   Discontent at the harvest

Trouble could arise ... when lords tried to introduce any reduction in the rights and benefits of the community. Thus in 1291, 'all the villeins of the township of Broughton ... went away from the great harvest boon [service], leaving their work from noon till night ... giving the malicious and false cause that they did not have their loaves as large as they were accustomed formerly, and ought to have them'.

From T. Williamson and E. Bellamy, *Property and Landscape*, 1987

Source E   A serious complaint against the Abbot

Sir Hugh de Fren, then justiciar of Chester, came to a place which is called Harebach Cross, at which a great number of villeins had taken refuge together, and they laid a serious complaint against the Abbot [their lord], that, whereas they were free and held their lands and tenements from aforetime by charter of the Lord the King, the Abbot ... had put them in close confinement in shackles, as though they were villeins, and forced them to serve him in all villein services ...

At length they returned to the Abbot, their lord, submitting themselves and their goods to his grace, and the Abbot put them all in fetters as his bondmen. and for many Sundays they stood in the choir, with bare heads and feet, and they offered wax candles in token of subjection.

From the Ledger Book of Vale Royal Abbey, 1336

Source F   The limitations of the manor courts

The manor courts were often powerless to redress wrongs. They normally dealt with such matters as disputes over labour service and trespass, with allegations of immorality and slander; they fined men for brawling or poaching, and punished girls for reducing their value by losing their virginity. But in years of unrest, there were more serious crimes to consider; and the manor courts were unable to deal with them.

From C. Hibbert, *The English*, 1994

The grievances of the peasantry

Sources **B** to **F** show that peasants did have an idea of their rights and were willing to defend them. They often failed to do so, however, and according to one historian 'the peasants who took the defence of ... their customary rights to the king's courts ... were usually defeated. Yet they came back time and again with assertions of their freedoms under the Crown even back to "the time of King Cnout".

In the 1300s peasants collected funds to pay for appeals to the Domesday Book so often that in the period before the great revolt in 1381, the gentry petitioned parliament against what they saw as a 'great rumour' or conspiracy of the peasantry. Most cases of violent resistance were localised and limited, but in 1381 popular resentment boiled over to create the Peasants' Revolt, which is the subject of a separate Case File (see pp. 38–9).

Questions

1. What evidence suggests that ordinary people could get justice in their local courts?

2. Why, therefore, do you think that the peasants in Source **E** failed in their claims?

3. Use your knowledge of law and society in medieval England to explain the problems referred to in Source **F**.

4. Using your knowledge of the period to help you interpret the evidence of Sources **B** to **F**, explain how far people could get justice in medieval England.

The Peasants' Revolt of 1381

▶ *What caused the peasants to rise in rebellion?*

The revolt was caused by a combination of long-term grievances and new oppression. The great plague known as the Black Death, and falling population, made labour scarce and valuable, but landlords still tried to enforce the old villein service. Attempts to collect a new poll tax led to demonstrations which ended with a march on London. The leaders of the revolt were Walter (Wat) Tyler and a radical priest named John Ball. The rebels attacked London and demanded a meeting with King Richard II. They did not challenge the King's authority but asked him to give them justice.

The King met the rebels at Mile End and promised to deal with their problems. He also pardoned them for their rebellion. Although some rebels left, a group led by Tyler entered the Tower of London and murdered the Archbishop of Canterbury and the Treasurer, Sir Robert Hales.

The next day the King met them again, but Tyler's behaviour provoked the Mayor of London so much that he killed him. King Richard calmed the rebels by promising pardons, but when they returned to their villages the pardons were used to identify them and they were hanged. However, the poll tax was not used again until the 1980s (when it had a similar effect). Sources **A** to **G** will help you to investigate the grievances that led to the outbreak of the revolt, and to assess what it achieved.

Source B Expectations for change

> The kindling for a general peasant revolt was there in the 1370s, and the resistance was for the first time born of hope, not of despair. After the Black Death, the basic relationship between land and people had at last changed. Social and economic freedom now seemed a practical possibility; an end to villeinage, free rents [rents without feudal services] at 2p an acre, and freely negotiable wage labour contracts. Rebellion might have come in any year after about 1377.
>
> From J.L. Bolton, *The Medieval English Economy, 1150–1500*, 1980

Source C The burden of the poll tax

> The cost of the Hundred Years War was more than the nation could bear. The king and his new parliament were desperate for money; even the crown jewels had been pawned. They thought up a poll tax – a personal tax on every individual in the country ... A levy of one groat [about 1.25p] was made on everybody over 14 years old. The proceeds were quickly spent on the war or absorbed by corruption. Then in 1380 a new poll tax of three groats per head over the age of fifteen was levied. Three groats was a considerable sum for a working man – almost a week's wages.
>
> Adapted from C. Poulsen, *The English Rebels*, 1984

Source A This illustration dates from 1390 and shows a peasant forced to carry a sack of hay and straw for his lord, a humiliating service

Source D A contemporary chronicle describes the demands made by Wat Tyler at Mile End

He asked that there should be no law in the realm save the law of king and parliament ... and that no lord should have lordship except civilly, and that there should be equality among all people save only the king, and that the goods of the Holy Church should not remain in the hands of the religious ... that clergy already in possession should have a sufficient sustenance [living] and the rest of the goods should be divided among the people of the parish ... and all lands and tenements now held by bishops should be confiscated and divided among the commons ... And he demanded that there should be no more villeins in England, and no serfdom or villeinage, but that all men should be free.

Source E The Peasants' Revolt: the death of Wat Tyler, with Richard II looking on (left); Richard II addressing his army (right)

Source F John Ball talking to the peasants

Source G The effect of the revolt

Did the revolt play any significant part in the development of English society in the following decades? The general view is that it was basic economic forces [the growth of trade, the shortage of labour] rather than events in 1381 which brought about the end of villeinage ... Certainly the suppression of the rising did not eliminate peasant unrest, although this went back to being a local problem, and in general to taking less violent forms. The most obvious casualty of the rising was the poll-tax, which was abandoned.

From J. Thomson, *The Transformation of Medieval England*, 1983

Questions

1 What grievances led to the Peasants' Revolt?

2 Was the revolt a crime? What crimes did the rebels commit?

3 Did the revolt achieve anything?

7 Crime and punishment, 1500–1750

Overview

 How did Britain change in this period?

A period of transformation

In 1485 Henry Tudor became king of a small English kingdom. His subjects were mainly farmers and a small, but growing, middle class of merchants, lawyers and officials. Literacy (the ability to read and write) was becoming more widespread, but education was still controlled by the Church. By 1750, Britain was the centre of a vast overseas empire, governed by a king and parliament who controlled the Church as well as laws, judges, taxes and people. This process of transformation provides the context for developments in the law and its enforcement, and for the changing nature of crime and punishment.

The period was one of great social and economic change. Source **A** shows how rapidly the population was expanding at this time. Trade expanded hugely and Britain became the wealthy centre of a worldwide empire. All this was achieved at the expense of many ordinary people. Rising prices meant hardship, and new farming methods brought the dividing and fencing of common land, called *enclosure*; many small farmers could not afford this and were reduced to working as landless labourers. The result was social unrest, eventually eased by the introduction of poor laws.

In 1536–42 a series of Acts of Union brought Wales within the English system of administration, and in 1603 the accession of James VI of Scotland as James I of England brought an end to the traditional rivalry of the English and Scottish crowns. The creation of the United Kingdom, with a single government, was completed by Acts of Union with Scotland in 1707, and Ireland in 1800.

Monarchy and parliament

In England, the power of the monarchy also changed a great deal. Like earlier monarchs Henry VII had two rivals for power: the wealthy barons and the Church. A system of *prerogative courts*, run by the king's council, enabled him to control even the most powerful lords, and in the 1530s Henry VIII seized control of the Church and its assets. This led to religious quarrels, and an increasing number of crimes relating to different religious beliefs. The struggle between Catholics and Protestants caused serious rebellion, and also led to persecution of individuals for the faith that they held.

Parliament (Source **B**) was used to make new laws, necessary for controlling the barons and the Church. These laws were added to the existing common law, and applied in the courts by the judges, and increasingly by justices of the peace. The responsibilities and power of these JPs increased throughout the sixteenth and seventeenth centuries – they were expected to deal with local crime, look after the roads and bridges, license and control inns and alehouses, and administer the system of poor laws when they developed.

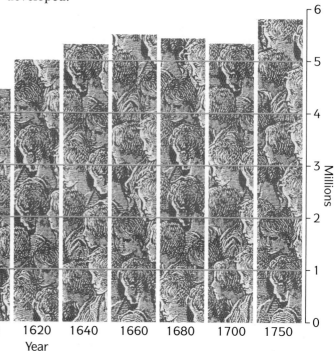

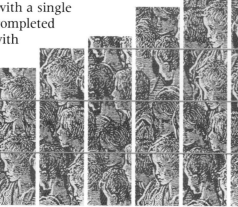
Source A
Graph of population rise

Year (x-axis): 1520, 1540, 1560, 1580, 1600, 1620, 1640, 1660, 1680, 1700, 1750
Millions (y-axis): 0, 1, 2, 3, 4, 5, 6

Source B
The parliament of Henry VIII

As the gentry grew in wealth and power, they sought the right to influence the king in parliament. In 1642 this quarrel exploded into civil war and it was clear that kings had to work with parliament. By the eighteenth century Britain had changed: the country was governed by a parliamentary and Protestant monarchy dominated by the nobility and the gentry.

Property or justice?

An essentially orderly society had been created, with an improving system of laws and courts, but it was one in which the protection of property and the rights of certain classes were more important than justice and injustice. Game laws and poachers, smugglers and highwaymen, transportation to the colonies and the Bloody Code (harsh laws and the death sentence for minor crimes) ran alongside the growth of manners, trade and empire.

Parliament made laws, but parliament represented the wealthy classes and made the laws they wanted. By the end of the eighteenth century new ideas were again challenging the system of politics and society, in the form of the French Revolution and the Industrial Revolution.

Questions

1 What changes occurred in Britain in this period in the following areas?
   a) Trade and farming **b)** Government **c)** Religion.

2 How did these changes affect the lives of ordinary people?

The enforcement of law

▶ *How was the King's Peace and the rule of law extended?*

By 1500 the system of law and courts in England was well established, but civil war in the fifteenth century had exposed some shortcomings, particularly the power of the nobility to disrupt the way it worked. Tudor monarchs wanted to ensure that the king's justice and the rule of law worked throughout the kingdom. This was done in a variety of ways, by passing new laws and establishing new courts.

New laws

New laws were passed through parliament, to exert control over the nobility. The most important were the Statute of Liveries of 1504 and the treason laws that followed the Reformation of the 1530s, when Henry VIII made himself head of the Church. The Statute of Liveries forbade the nobility to keep private armies dressed in their own uniform, or livery, while the treason laws made it treason to speak or write against the king. These laws allowed the early Tudor monarchs to control powerful lords who might threaten them. They also allowed people to be prosecuted for their religious beliefs if they undermined the king's authority.

The Star Chamber

New courts which operated by the king's *prerogative* (personal authority) were established. They were run by judges who were members of the king's Privy Council, and did not have juries. The king was therefore able to impose his authority and will on the nobility in a way that sheriffs, county courts and even the assizes had found difficult. The most famous of them was the Court of the Star Chamber, which was established in 1487 (see Source **A**).

Later, however, the power of the Star Chamber came to be used differently. One of the most famous cases dealt with in the Star Chamber involved three Puritans (extreme Protestants) named Burton, Bastwick and Prynne. They had published a pamphlet which attacked Charles I's religious policies. They also criticised the Queen, who was a Roman Catholic. In 1637 they were sentenced by the Star Chamber

to be placed in the pillory, then to have their ears clipped. The shocked crowd were angry both because they sympathised with what the three had said, but also because sentences of mutilation were not used against members of the gentry (see Source **B**).

Source A The purpose of the Star Chamber

A widespread cause of crime was the use barons made of their private armies of retainers [followers] dressed in their livery. But how was a powerful man with his retainers to be tamed? The answer ... was a strong court in London where a powerful man would not be able to make use of his local influence, where there was no jury to corrupt, and where torture, not allowed in the common-law courts, could be used against anyone accused of a crime.

The so-called Star Chamber was simply the King's Council meeting on Wednesdays and Fridays from 9 a.m. to 11 a.m. in the Star Chamber to do judicial business ... People could be summoned to it by writs. It dealt with matters not properly covered by Acts of Parliament or the common law; its punishments were not controlled by acts, but as the court thought fit. They ranged from heavy fines to pillorying, ear-cropping, nose-slitting, branding and whipping, but not the death penalty.

From R. Whiting, *Crime and Punishment*, 1986

Source B A cartoon showing Laud supposedly dining on Prynne's ears after the famous Star Chamber case of 1637. Many cartoons like this were later published against the government, and against Archbishop of Canterbury Laud in particular.

The prerogative courts came to be resented because they favoured the king over local interests, and because they were used to silence criticism from people like Puritans. They were eventually abolished by parliament in 1641. The legal system was then once more dominated by the common law.

Problems on the borders

The problems created by robber barons were especially serious on the borders of the kingdom (see Source **C**). Although Edward I had effectively conquered Wales, royal authority was remote, symbolised by the castles he left behind him. The lands bordering England were controlled by 'Marcher lords'. In many ways they ruled as local princes, able to use the law for their own purposes. Similar powers had been given to lords in the North of England, who were required to protect England from invasion by the Scots. The result was that law and order was difficult to maintain.

Source C Anarchy in the Borders

Between England and Scotland there was prolonged and terrible violence, and ... the Border country suffered fearfully in the process ... Armies marched and counter-marched and fought and fled across it; it was wasted, burned and despoiled, its people harried, robbed and slaughtered, on both sides, by both sides.

From G.M. Fraser, *The Steel Bonnets*, 1971

Juries were unable to convict Marcher lords, and if they were fined for any crimes they would hold a meeting called a *commortha* where they collected the money from the people that they governed. Edward IV was able to confiscate some of the lordships from those who had fought (and died) on the losing side in the Wars of the Roses; one of these was the the most powerful of all, the Mortimer lordship. Henry VII and Henry VIII continued the practice. Prerogative councils for the North and Welsh Marches improved the situation (see Source **D**), but the eventual solution to the problem was the creation of a single United Kingdom. The essential steps were the Acts of Union between England and Wales in the reign of Henry VIII, and the union of the English and Scottish crowns at the accession of James VI of Scotland as James I of England in 1603 (see Source **E**). (Ireland was treated separately because it had no common land border with the other kingdoms; it was not fully integrated into the United Kingdom until the Act of Union of 1800.)

Source D The work of Rowland Lee

Rowland Lee, the Bishop of Lichfield and Coventry, was made President of the Council for Wales in 1534, with power to order executions. Although a clergyman, he had never preached and preferred to lead his men chasing cattle thieves. As a brutal, fearless and energetic man, he was ideal for the job in Henry's eyes; he enjoyed punishing criminals ... He had the help of a number of emergency laws declared by the king, including night-time curfews, the right to punish juries who brought in false verdicts, and to take criminals from the Marches for trial. The chronicler, Ellis Griffith, claimed that he hanged 5000 in six years.

From R. Whiting, *Crime and Punishment*, 1986

Source E
A portrait of James I

When James became king of England in 1603, he declared that the borders of England and Scotland were the centre of his kingdom. This began a drive to destroy the power of the 'reivers', criminal gangs who operated on both sides of the border. New wardens were appointed who co-operated in rounding up known offenders. By 1604, 32 reivers had been hanged, 15 more banished and 140 outlawed. In 1605 a new commission was appointed, and by 1610 the power of the reiver clans was broken.

Questions

1 What evidence suggests that the Star Chamber encouraged greater justice?

2 How had the use of the Star Chamber changed by the 1630s?

3 Why do you think it was abolished in 1641?

4 Why did law enforcement in the border areas improve in the sixteenth and early seventeenth centuries? What part did the prerogative courts play in this?

5 Using all the evidence and your knowledge of the period, explain why the prerogative courts outlived their usefulness.

Improving law enforcement

How was the law enforced?

Source A A judge on circuit. Judges travelled to counties to hold assizes, where serious crimes had been referred by the JPs.

The justices of the peace

Tudor monarchs asserted their control by shifting power away from the sheriffs to the JPs who were appointed and supervised by the Privy Council. Their powers and functions increased steadily, and they took on responsibility for administration and law enforcement as well as for local law courts at the petty and quarter sessions. As Sources **A**, **B** and **C** show, they were a vital part of a hierarchy (ladder) of law courts which ended in the central courts at Westminster, controlled by councillors and judges who directly represented the king himself. Source **D** illustrates the more serious kinds of crime with which they dealt – even if the case passed to the assizes, JPs were usually involved in the early stages.

Source B The power of JPs

JPs had considerable powers. A justice acting on his own could ... examine and imprison suspected felons, arrest vagabonds and rogues, stop affrays, arrest recusants (those who refused to attend their parish church, normally because they were Catholics) and take bonds for good behaviour from those accused of bad. Two justices together could ... fix the poor rate, grant alehouse licences, supervise the repair of roads and bridges, take bail and decide on paternity in cases of bastardy. But it was at the quarter sessions ... that the justices exercised most power. In these courts they sat as judges, assisted in criminal trials by a grand jury [who decided if there was a case to answer] and trial juries [who decided if the accused was guilty]. Once an individual had been convicted it was the justices who determined within the law what punishment should be imposed.

From J. Briggs et al., *Crime and Punishment in England*, 1996

Source C From the Notebook of Sir William Bromley, a Warwickshire JP who kept records of his out-of-session work

1691 7 Feb. On the complaint of ... Norton of Kenilworth, mercer, that his daughter Sarah lives an idle, disorderly life and pilfers his goods. Sir W. Broughton and I committed her to the house of correction.
1691 8 May. Alexander Barlow of Brincklow, alehousekeeper, swore the peace against Gervase Ledgely of the same, carpenter, for beating him and threatening to burn his house.

Source D Table of felonies in Elizabethan Essex

Offences	Number
Against the person	
Rape and buggery	19 (2%)
Witchcraft	71 (7%)
Murder and homicide	71 (7%)
Against property	
Burglary, robbery and forcible entry	170 (18%)
Theft	637 (66%)
Total	968

From J. Briggs et al., *Crime and Punishment in England*, 1996

Unlike the sheriff, the JPs were readily available in most villages, and were able to arrest and commit a criminal to begin proceedings. Minor offences could be dealt with on the spot, others at the sessions or assizes. They also played a crucial part in crime prevention, since they were responsible for the licensing and regulation of alehouses (often considered the source of much crime and corruption) and the operation of the vagrancy and poor laws. Most importantly they supervised a hierarchy of peace-keeping officials who operated at village and parish levels. Source **E** illustrates the role of these officials and their relationship to one another.

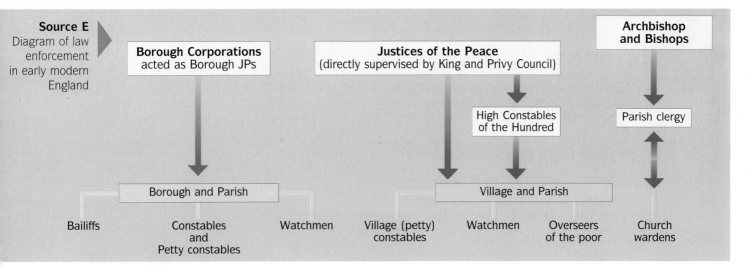

Source E
Diagram of law enforcement in early modern England

Borough Corporations acted as Borough JPs	Justices of the Peace (directly supervised by King and Privy Council)	Archbishop and Bishops

High Constables of the Hundred

Parish clergy

Borough and Parish	Village and Parish

Bailiffs | Constables and Petty constables | Watchmen | Village (petty) constables | Watchmen | Overseers of the poor | Church wardens

Manor courts and church courts

In addition, the older manor and church courts continued to deal with minor crime. However, people's attitudes to these courts differed, as Sources **F** to **H** illustrate. Source **I** helps to explain why.

Source F   The survival of the manor courts

The manor courts survived because they met a need. The jury consisted of local peasant landholders, and ale-tasters, tithingmen and/or a constable presented offenders to the court. Punishments were nearly always fines. A large number of villagers were involved as officials of the court, and penalties were enforceable. If a defendant failed to pay a fine, the bailiff seized goods to the correct value. The final sanction of the court was to dispossess the peasant of his land.

Adapted from J. Briggs et al., *Crime and Punishment in England*, 1996

Source G   A contemporary view of the church courts, taken from a text published in 1641

Source H   The role of the church courts

The role of the Church courts was not to punish but to reform people; to reconcile them with God and their neighbours. They have been called the 'Bawdy Courts' because so many of their cases related to sexual offences, but they did a great deal more than this. There were complaints of interference, and many of their decisions were ignored, but they did represent common opinion, and many cases were initiated by members of the community rather than churchwardens and officials.

From J. Briggs et al., *Crime and Punishment in England*, 1996

Source I   Crimes reported in church courts

Case 1, from 1598 Upon Sunday before Michaelmas in time of afternoon service, William Haynes of Southbemfleet was dancing with minstrels on a green by Thomas Harris his house.
Case 2, from 1599 Thomas Ward, of Purleigh, was presented as by report, to seek help at a sorcerer's hands. Confessed that, having lost certain cattle … he went to one Taylor in Thaxted, a wizard, to know whether they were bewitched, and to have his help.
Case 3, from 1600 Thomas Perrin of Rayleigh reported for a common drunkard and railer and chider, to the grief of the Godly and great danger to his soul.

Questions

1 What were the advantages of the manor courts? How does this explain their survival?

2 What sort of crimes were dealt with in the church courts?

3 What do you think Source **G** is trying to say? Does Source **H** suggest that this is a fair criticism?

4 If their decisions were often ignored, why do you think church courts still existed?

8 Crime and society, 1500–1750

Poverty and disorder

 Why did more people fear crime?

A change in the attitude to crime

Society was becoming increasingly respectable, affluent and law-abiding in this period, but it also seems to have become increasingly concerned with crime and the threat of disorder. Source **A** gives evidence to support this view.

Source A The protection of privilege

Between 1485 and 1660 there was a significant change in both attitudes to and the perception of crime in England. In the early part of this period it was the aristocrats and their armed retainers who threatened the kingdom. On the whole common people did not present a serious threat. By 1660, disorder among, and crimes by, the common people were increasingly seen as threats to society. The protection of order and the protection of privilege were seen as the same thing, and the criminal law became increasingly an instrument of social control.

Adapted from J. Briggs et al., *Crime and Punishment in England*, 1996

Source B Sheep farming

Source C
A seventeenth-century woodcut of a beggar

We saw in the previous chapter how the threat of the nobility was dealt with, and how the 'respectable' middle classes came to play their part in law enforcement. The improvements in law enforcement would have been impossible without their co-operation, and those who had possessions and property to protect felt an increasing identity with those who had the authority to protect them. Why was it that they were coming to see crime as a threat, and especially as a threat coming from the lower classes?

Hard times for the poor

The growth of population led to rising prices and plenty of labour, so that wages could not keep pace. Rising prices also encouraged landlords to raise rents. Tenants who could not pay had their holdings taken over and exploited as part of the lord's estate. With more people to feed, farmers were encouraged to use more land to farm. Often land traditionally used as common or waste land was enclosed and brought under cultivation. Poorer villagers who relied on this land were thereby deprived of an essential part of their income. In addition, the growth of the wool trade encouraged sheep farming (see Source **B**) which required much less labour. Unemployment and hardship was often the result, as shown in Source **C**.

Beggars and vagabonds

Lack of employment and income led to robbery and theft. Riots occurred when villagers protested against enclosures. Popular discontent led to rebellion, occasionally in a spontaneous outbreak such as Kett's Rebellion in 1549. Perhaps most disturbing to the authorities were the bands of 'sturdy beggars' and rogues who roamed the countryside in search of work or other sources of income.

Sources **D** to **G** focus on the nature and extent of the problem, but to understand why it created such fear, you need to remember the nature of society. There was no police force to keep order; order had traditionally been achieved by small, known communities and local lords. Society had always been threatened by those who lived outside this structure, for example as outlaws, but the vagabonds were not separated from society as outlaws were, and were far more numerous.

In addition, the growing influence of a Protestant religion placed great emphasis on personal morality and hard work. The idea of predestination put forward by a French reformer, John Calvin, drew a sharp distinction between the 'saints' who lived respectably and would go to heaven, and the sinful multitude. This made it easy to see the idle and criminal as sinful – wicked as well as dangerous.

Source F Sixteenth-century beggars

Source D Types of rogues

The rogues are of two main types: the filthy ragged vagabonds who roam about begging and stealing, and the smartly dressed and cunning tricksters, mostly in London and a few large towns. Of the roaming vagabonds there are: the masterful 'Upright men', the leaders of the gangs; bullying 'Rufflers' who beg from the strong and rob the weak; 'Hookers' and 'Anglers' who steal from open windows by hooked poles; 'Palliards, Counterfeit Cranks, Dommerers and Abraham men' who present themselves as sick, deformed or mad.

Adapted from Thomas Harman, *Caveat for Common Cursetors*, 1568

Source E Types of vagabonds

'Jarckmen' forge licences to beg. 'Curtsey-men' will go commonly well-apparelled [dressed] without any weapon, and in places where they meet together in their hostelries they will bear the part of right good gentlemen ... but commonly they will pay them with stealing a pair of sheets or coverlet. All are followed by 'Doxies', women broken and spoiled of their maidenhead, 'Dells', young wenches not yet broken, 'Walking Morts [whores], Kynchin Coes and Kynchin Morts' [children] and 'Bawdy Baskets' who are female pedlars selling trifles.

From John Audley, *Fraternity of Vagabonds*, 1561

Source G The scale of the problem

It is difficult to be precise about the actual numbers of beggars and vagabonds. In 1577 William Harrison wrote, 'It is not yet full three-score years since this trade began, but how it hath prospered since that time is easie to judge ... to amount unto about 10,000 persons.' Other estimates put the numbers much higher. In 1594 the Lord Mayor of London suggested there were as many as 12,000 beggars in the city alone; and in 1569 constables searched throughout the country and apprehended 13,000 rogues and masterless men.

Adapted from C. Hibbert, *The English*, 1994

Questions

1 Which of the beggars described in Sources **D** and **E** do you think are pictured in Source **F**?

2 What do these descriptions suggest to you about: **a)** the beggars and their lives; **b)** the attitude of those who wrote about them?

3 Given the nature of sixteenth-century society, how accurate do you think the estimates of numbers in Source **G** would be?

4 How far do you think that the evidence provided by these sources can offer an accurate picture of the problem of 'sturdy beggars'?

Crime, poverty and the poor laws

▶ *How did governments respond to poverty and disorder?*

Tudor governments responded to the problems of poverty and disorder with a variety of short-term measures. Initially they defined crimes more strictly and punished them more harshly (see Source **A**). Gradually, however, there seems to have been a deeper recognition of the problems created by poverty as well as idleness, requiring special measures. These developed into a system of poor laws, designed to care for the needy, to punish the idle and, above all, to keep control (see Sources **B** to **D**).

Source A
Punishments were harsh ▶

It seems reasonable to treat as 'crimes' all actions which might lead to prosecution in the secular [civil] or ecclesiastical courts, while recognising that felonies – treason, murder, grand larceny [major theft] – were set apart, by carrying the death penalty, from such lesser offences. During the sixteenth century, the attitudes of rulers hardened towards crime … Their fears were reflected in legislation [new laws]. Under the first two Tudors, several offences had become felonies by statute such as hunting at night or abduction of women. Some of the statutes were repealed under Edward, but revived under Elizabeth. Punishments were harsh: traitors were hanged, cut down while still alive, and disembowelled; felons, who might in law have done no more than steal goods worth 12d [5p], were hanged by slow strangulation; lesser offenders were branded, mutilated, whipped, or sent to the galleys.

From P. Williams, *The Later Tudors*, 1995

Source B A vagabond being whipped through the streets

Source C Bridewell, originally built as a palace, but given to London by Edward VI in 1553 as a workhouse and house of correction for the poor. The name Bridewell came to be used as a nickname for a house of correction.

Source D From the town records of Ipswich

Wednesday 2 Dec. 1551 – Two in every parish shall be nominated by the bailiffs to enquire into the poor of the parish.
Monday 22 Feb. 1557 – No children of this town shall be permitted to beg. Those adults that shall be permitted to beg shall have badges.
Monday 26 Sept. 1569 – The late house of Blackfriars, bought of John Southwell, shall be henceforth a hospital for the poor people of this town, and shall be called Christ's Hospital.

Source E From the Middlesex Records, 1573

29March 1573 – At Harrow Hill in Middlesex, John Allan, Elizabeth Turner, Humphrey Foxe, Henry Bower and Agnes Vat, being over 14 years of age and having no lawful means of livelihood, were declared vagabonds. Sentenced to be flogged and burned through the right ear.

The legislation

In 1531 and 1547, parliament passed Acts enabling vagrants (wandering beggars) to be punished by flogging and returning them to their own parish, and later by branding them. In 1572 a new Act authorised JPs to collect a weekly rate from each parish to provide help to the old, sick or disabled poor, and to punish the able-bodied or vagrants who had no work (see Source **E**). In 1576 the government ordered 'houses of correction' to be built in all towns, where the idle could be housed, set to work and kept under control.

In 1598 and 1601 two new Acts created a more coherent system. Each parish was to have 'overseers of the poor', whose job was to establish a register of the poor, collect a weekly tax from the wealthier residents and distribute it according to need. The old and disabled were given help, but only within their own parish. Those who were able-bodied were set to work, and pauper children were apprenticed to learn a trade. (See Sources **F** and **G**.)

Source F From the 1598 poor law

Be it enacted, that the churchwardens of every parish and four well-off house-owners ... shall be called overseers of the poor. They shall ... set to work the children of all parents who shall not ... be thought able to keep and support their children, and also all persons who, married or unmarried, having no means to maintain them, use no ordinary and daily trade of life to get their living by.

Source G
From the town records of Norwich, 1598–9

Total money collected for poor relief – £110 4s 4d
Payments made:

Paid to the poor according to the weekly assessment	£56	3s	10d
Paid to the extremely sick	2	7s	3d
Paid for making Kindlemarsh's child an apprentice	3	0s	0d
Paid for keeping Clarke's child	1	18s	4d
Paid for nursing a young infant left in the parish one week		1s	8d
Paid for naming and arranging for vagrant child born in parish	2	11s	4d
Paid to constables for sending away vagabonds		4s	8d
Paid to the overseers of St Myhelles	12	5s	0d
Paid to the overseers of St Giles		8s	0d

*Q*uestions

1 What methods of dealing with the poor are shown in Sources **D** and **E**?

2 Use this information to explain what is happening in Source **B**.

3 What attitudes are shown towards poverty and the poor in these sources?

4 Does Source **G** prove that the law of 1598 (Source **F**) was carried out in practice?

5 What evidence shows that the poor were:
a) helped, **b)** punished, and **c)** controlled?
Use your knowledge of the period to explain why they were treated in this way.

London: a criminal underworld

 What were the effects of the increasingly harsh laws?

The problem of debt

The poor laws eased the effects of poverty, assisted by a reduction in the rate of population increase after 1650. But vagrancy led to a permanent change in attitudes towards crime and criminals: the criminal was now associated with idleness and moral weakness. This harsh attitude led to harsh punishment: for example, those who got into debt were imprisoned until their debts were paid.

Since they could not then earn a living, this practice often led to destitution for debtors and their families, and did nothing to repay the money to those it was owed to. Some criminals exploited the law and paid gaolers for a comfortable cell while avoiding their creditors. But many could not afford to do this and rotted in prison. Complaints about the law on debt became increasingly common in the seventeenth century, as Sources **A** and **B** illustrate.

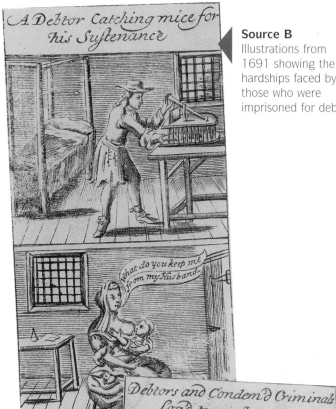

Source B
Illustrations from 1691 showing the hardships faced by those who were imprisoned for debt

Source A From 'A Remonstrance of Many Thousand Citizens', a Leveller petition to parliament written by Richard Overton in 1646

Ye know also, imprisonment for debt is not from the beginning; yet ye think not of these many thousand persons and families that are destroyed thereby; ye are rich and abound in goods, and have need of nothing, but the afflictions of the poor, your hunger-starved brethren, ye have no compassion of.

Crime in London

In the larger towns a professional, criminal underworld was now developing, and London was one of the worst such affected areas. With its maze of narrow streets and alleyways, wealthy inhabitants and visitors, and shifting population, London had always attracted a criminal element, as Source **C** shows. But the city had grown enormously as a result of trade, as Source **D** demonstrates, and it is not surprising that it attracted those more interested in the rich pickings of crime than genuine work. Crime was widespread and the appropriate punishments harsh and often immediate (see Sources **E** and **F**).

Source C A description of twelfth-century London, written by a monk from Winchester

When you reach England, if you come to London, pass through it quickly. No one lives in it without falling into some sort of crime. Every quarter of it abounds with grave obscenities. Whatever evil or malicious thing that can be found in any part of the world, you will find it in that one city. Actors, jesters, smooth-skinned lads, Moors, flatterers, pretty boys, effeminates, pederasts, singing and dancing girls, quacks, belly-dancers, sorceresses, extortioners, night wanderers, magicians, mimes, beggars, buffoons: all this tribe fill all the houses. Therefore, if you do not want to dwell with evildoers do not live in London.

Source D Population table showing the rapid growth that took place in London from 1500 to 1750

Year	London	Norwich
1500	50,000	10,000
1600	200,000	20,000
1650	400,000	30,000
1665	500,000	30,000
1700	550,000	32,000
1750	750,000	35,000

From P. Sauvain, *Changing World*, 1992

Source E Widespread crime and rapid punishment

As well as treason and heresy there were many other serious crimes associated with Tudor London. It would seem that murder was not uncommon. Punishment could follow swiftly on the act. The murderers of two Italians were tried, convicted and hanged a mere five days after the offence. A prisoner on trial at the Old Bailey pulled a knife and killed another in court. For this murder he was summarily convicted and taken outside, the hand that struck the blow was amputated, and he was hanged on improvised gallows. A multitude of other offences, such as coin-clipping, rape, horse theft, cutpursing and the theft of any item valued at 40 shillings or more, were subject to the death penalty.

Adapted from J. Briggs et al., *Crime and Punishment in England*, 1996

Source F A woodcut illustrating the cutpurse John Selman; this sort of crime was widespread in London

Questions

1 Look at Sources **A** and **B**.
a) Why did Overton think that the treatment was unjust? **b)** How does Source **B** support his arguments?

2 Look at Sources **C** to **F**.
a) Why should London be associated so closely with crime? **b)** Source **C** suggests that this wasn't new. Does this mean that London had not changed?

3 Why were such harsh punishments used? Do the sources suggest that they were effective?

Crimes and scandals

By the late sixteenth century there was a highly organised criminal underworld in London, and by the mid-seventeenth century the activities of these criminals were widely publicised. Printing had become much more widespread and this allowed pamphlets to be published in large numbers. Also, restrictions on printing had decreased during the Civil War and illegal presses became well established. Some rules were reimposed after 1660, but printers were able to produce graphic accounts of scandals and crimes, as shown in Source **G**.

Source G   Title page from the 'Bloody Newes From Dover', 1647

While pamphlets related crimes from all over England, such as the serial murders at Gloucester in 'The Bloody Innkeeper' (1675) and the Dover incident seen in Source **A**, London remained the source of most horror stories. The career of 'Country Tom and Canterbury Bess' (see Source **H**) seemed to illustrate all the dangers of the city, to victims and potential criminals alike. However, some historians have suggested that, colourful though the London underworld may have been, it did not constitute a serious threat to society. Consider the views expressed in Source **I**, and then use all the sources and the Rogues Gallery to decide how far you agree.

Source H   Country Tom and Canterbury Bess

The most celebrated case of the period was of Thomas Sherwood and Elizabeth Evans, known as Country Tom and Canterbury Bess. They devised a simple routine in which Bess would pick up a man, preferably drunk, at a playhouse or tavern and lure him to a dark spot where Tom would club and rob him. On the evening of April 1st 1635, Bess picked up one Thomas Claxton, gentleman, and lured him to Grays Inn Fields, where Tom killed him and stripped the body naked. A milkmaid found it next morning; a watch was set, and Tom gave the pair away by trying to sell the dead man's clothes. Dispatched to Newgate prison, they quickly confessed to both Claxton's murder and two others.

Adapted from *History Today*, 1996

Source I   Features of crime in London

There are three important features of crime in early modern London. First, most offenders were not professional criminals and the criminal problem, even in the capital, was not primarily organised crime. Secondly there seems to have been a lot of crime, especially as the cases recorded refer to convictions and do not record unsuccessful prosecutions or unreported crime. Thirdly there are few contemporary expressions of fear. Londoners seemed to be able to live with their criminals.

Adapted from J. Briggs et al., *Crime and Punishment in England*, 1996

Source J   The London underworld was highly organised

The London underworld was more highly organised than the policing system of the day. Some parts, such as 'Damnation Alley' and 'Devil's Gap', were 'safe' areas for criminals. The criminal brotherhood saw to the allocation of tasks, operational areas, disposal of stolen goods and the systematic training of recruits ... Pamphlets were frequently issued to warn country visitors to London of these people. When walking in St. Paul's Cathedral 'approach not within 5 fathom of that pillar but bend your course directly to the middle line.' Cutpurses used to hide behind pillars.

From R. Whiting, *Crime and Punishment*, 1986

In 1678 anti-Catholic prejudice of the period led to rumours of a so-called Popish Plot and several anti-Catholic riots. The plot was invented by a rogue named Titus Oates, but was made to appear genuine when the Justice to whom he revealed it, Sir Edmund Berry Godfrey, was murdered a few days later. In fact, the murder was the work of common rogues and those executed for the crime were almost certainly innocent.

Source K Playing cards showing the murder of Sir Edmund Berry Godfrey in 1678

Jonathan Wild, 'Thief Taker General'

Rogues gallery

Jonathan Wild, 1683–1725

Wild was a minor law officer in London, who set up a lost property office in 1713 but was, in fact, in contact with thieves who brought him stolen items. These were later returned to the owners for a reward. He also gained control of the London gangs, through force and blackmail. He arrested anyone not under his control and awarded himself the title of 'Thief Taker General of Great Britain and Ireland'. He divided London into different areas, each given to a particular gang, and pinned the blame for their robberies on those who refused to accept his control. By 1722 he had become rich and famous, and even the Privy Council asked for his advice to stop the growth of highway robberies. He inspired growing resentment within the underworld, and eventually investigations revealed a property swindle. Found guilty of receiving stolen goods, he was executed at Tyburn in 1725. He has been described as 'the first modern gangster'.

Jack Sheppard, 1702–24

Jack Sheppard was a petty thief skilled at picking locks. When his girlfriend, Edgworth Bess, was arrested, he rescued her, and when they were both arrested in 1724, he got them both out of the New Prison. Later, he and Blueskin Blake were arrested by Jonathan Wild for theft, but they escaped from Newgate Prison by cutting away a cell bar after Bess smuggled in some tools. Wild had Bess arrested and tortured to make her talk, and he was soon captured. Back in Newgate he became a celebrity when he escaped from his own chains, got through six iron-barred doors and reached the roof. He then returned to his cell for blankets which he used to lower himself to a nearby house roof. He was free for ten days before being recaptured while drunk. Sheppard was kept in his cell in 300 lb chains, but he was still able to entertain the public and have his portrait painted. The gaolers charged the public to see him, and in fact public sympathy for Jack helped in

the downfall of Wild. Eventually Sheppard was executed, taking fifteen minutes to die, in front of 250,000 people. Blueskin was also executed, and Bess was transported.

Dick Turpin, died 1739

The famous highwayman was not the romantic character his legend suggests. Beginning as a butcher selling stolen animals as meat, he fled when his crimes were discovered and joined a gang in Essex. Later he operated from a cave in Epping Forest with a highwayman, Tom King. In 1737 he shot at two people in a coach, but missed, and knowing that he could now be recognised, fled to Yorkshire. The story that he rode there in record time is false: it refers to a thief named Nevison who robbed a sailor in Kent and then rode to York in sixteen hours (it took three days by coach) in order to establish an alibi. Nevertheless, he was later identified and hanged. Turpin worked in Yorkshire as a horse-dealer under the name of John Palmer, but was arrested in 1739 when he threatened to shoot a neighbour. He was identified and hanged at York.

Questions

1 In what ways does the evidence in the sources and the Rogues Gallery:
a) support the claims made in Source **C**, and b) contradict the claims made in Source **I**?

2 Why might this evidence give a false impression of crime in London?

3 How would most people know about crime and criminals in London?

4 Some of the more famous criminals became celebrities. Does this mean that people in London admired criminals?

5 What does the evidence suggest about how crime tends to be reported?

9 Crime and religion, 1500–1750

The early Tudors and the Church

 What was persecution?

The Reformation

Religion was very important in early modern England as most people believed in God, heaven and hell. People also believed that the Church could care for their souls, but this meant that the Church could be used to control people's behaviour and attitudes. We have already seen this in the role of the church courts, but the Church also had an important political role: to tell people their place in life and to obey those in power over them. Source **A** shows these kinds of attitudes.

Source A An Elizabethan homily on obedience, of the kind frequently read out in church services

Almighty God hath created and appointed all things in heaven, earth and waters in a most excellent and perfect order. In heaven He hath appointed distinct orders and states of archangels and angels. In earth, He hath appointed kings, princes, with other governors under them, in all good and necessary order … Every degree of people in their vocation, calling and office hath appointed to them their duty and order: some are high in degree, some are low.

For centuries this system had worked, based on a partnership between the monarchy and the Roman Catholic Church headed by the Pope. This had given the Church wealth and power, but many people resented this, feeling that priests should pay more attention to spiritual duties. One example of this was the Lollards in the Peasants' Revolt of 1381 (see pp. 38–9). By the 1520s, criticism of the Church was high across Europe, and a German monk, Martin Luther, challenged the Pope in what became the Protestant Reformation.

The Burning of Wm Coker, Wm Hopper, H.Laurence, R.Colliar, R.Wright & Wm Stere, at Canterbury.

Source B A sixteenth-century illustration showing the punishment of Protestants for heresy – the crime of speaking out against the Church

Henry VIII

Matters grew worse when in 1529 King Henry VIII wanted to divorce his wife, Catherine of Aragon, in order to marry Anne Boleyn. The Pope refused to grant a divorce so Henry used Protestant ideas, and a widespread anti-clerical feeling in England, to take control of the Church. He did so by the Act of Supremacy in 1534, which declared the King head of the Church of England. New treason laws also made it a crime to support the Pope. When the Bishop of Rochester, John Fisher, and the King's Chancellor, Sir Thomas More, who is pictured in Source **C**, refused to accept this, both were executed as traitors.

Henry VIII intended these changes mainly to increase his power and wealth, but the changes also began a century of religious division in England by making various beliefs and activities a crime. This was not new – heretics had always been treated as criminals – but the practice was now more widespread and more intense. As the king had the right to choose the doctrines of the Church, if you believed differently you had to choose between loyalty to the monarchy and loyalty to God. If you chose loyalty to God you could be accused of committing treason.

Source C
A portrait of Sir Thomas More by the artist Holbein

Source D   The Pilgrimage of Grace

The pilgrims were northerners, rich and poor, men and women. Many had lost jobs in monasteries or on monastery farms. The poorest had depended on the monks for food and money. Now they wondered how they would survive. Others joined the rebellion because they did not want to leave the Catholic Church.

From C. Maltman and I. Dawson, *The Making of the UK*, 1992

Source E   Map showing the number and distribution of burnings in England during Mary's reign (1553–8)

Key
Number of people burnt in each area

Henry rejected the Pope's power, but he did not make great changes to church services, so many people could easily accept what was happening. However, between 1536 and 1539 he closed down the abbeys and monasteries, which had special links with Rome. Those who resisted were executed, and a rebellion in the North in 1536, the Pilgrimage of Grace, was brutally suppressed (see Source **D**). To do all this Henry needed the support of English Protestants, and so he allowed the Bible to be translated into English, so that people could read it for themselves.

Mary Tudor

Henry also had his son, Edward, educated by Protestants – and when Edward became king in 1547, Protestant ideas began to flourish. But Edward died in 1553 and Mary, the daughter of Catherine of Aragon, became queen, and immediately restored the power of the Pope. Protestants were forced to leave England or meet secretly, and those who were caught were burned as heretics (see Sources **B** and **E**).

By Mary's death in 1558 over 300 people had been executed, including bishops and priests as well as many ordinary people. The English people were not used to persecution and Mary soon became deeply unpopular. In 1554 Sir Thomas Wyatt led a rebellion to try to put Mary's sister, Elizabeth, on the throne. Matters were made worse when England was dragged into a war with France to help Spain, and lost her last remaining French possession, the town of Calais. By 1558 many English people had come to fear and hate both Spain and the Catholic Church.

Questions

1 Why did Tudor monarchs want to control the Church?

2 Why did they make it a crime to have different religious beliefs?

The Church and the persecution of Catholics

 Why did Catholics become so unpopular?

Source A The execution of Mary, Queen of Scots

Elizabeth's attempt at compromise

England was divided over religion when Elizabeth became queen in 1558. She tried to find a compromise by establishing an Anglican ('English') Church somewhere between the Catholic and Protestant positions. A Protestant Church of England kept on some of the familiar Catholic services and symbols because people knew and liked them. Elizabeth hoped that both Catholics and Protestants would live together in her Church.

Although this worked for some people, persecutions had left two extreme groups who could not accept the compromise. Strong Protestants wanted to remove all traces of Catholicism, believing that they would corrupt the Church. They became known as 'Puritans'. Although mostly loyal to the Queen, their attempts to use parliament to make further changes led to quarrels in the reigns of both Elizabeth and James I. Extreme Catholics, on the other side, wanted to restore the Pope's power and destroy Protestant ideas.

Persecution again

In 1570 the Pope excommunicated Elizabeth (expelled her from the Catholic Church), and declared it the duty of Catholics to kill her and replace her with her Catholic cousin, Mary, Queen of Scots. There were many plots against Elizabeth which led to further persecution of Catholics, and eventually to the execution of Mary in 1587. Sources **A** to **C** illustrate these developments. In addition, these events and the government propaganda about them confirmed Puritan fears, so by the early seventeenth century anti-Catholic prejudice was a normal part of English life.

Catholics were not always treated as criminals because of their beliefs. Under Elizabeth it was compulsory to attend church on Sundays, and those who refused could be fined as 'recusants'. After 1570, however, government persecution concentrated on Catholic priests, especially those who had trained in France and Spain to carry out missionary work in England. These were hunted down and punished as traitors. This meant that they could be tortured and then hanged, drawn and quartered. Persecution was most rigorous at times when a plot had been discovered, or when there was a particular danger such as the threat of Spanish invasion in the 1580s.

Source B How Catholics were treated early in the reign of Elizabeth

The majority of Elizabeth's subjects obediently attended church services on Sundays, if only to avoid the shilling fine for non-attendance. Catholicism remained strongest in those areas most distant from central government, such as the North and West. In some ways the house with a domestic chaplain became a kind of religious community in which children, servants and tenants alike attended services. The vast majority of these people remained loyal to Elizabeth, and until the Catholic earls rebelled in 1568–9 Elizabeth treated her Catholic subjects leniently.

Adapted from G. Regan, *Elizabeth I*, 1988

Source C From the papal bull (order of the Pope) excommunicating Elizabeth I, 1570

Elizabeth, the pretended Queen of England, the servant of wickedness ... having seized on the kingdom and monstrously usurped the place of Supreme Head of the Church in all England ... hath again reduced the said kingdom into a miserable and ruinous condition, which was so lately reclaimed to the Catholic faith and a thriving condition ... [We] do out of the fullness of Our Apostolic power declare the aforesaid Elizabeth as being an heretic and a favourer of heretics ... and to be cut off from the unity of the Body of Christ [the Church]. And moreover, we do declare her to be deprived of her pretended title to the kingdom aforesaid ... and also the nobility, subjects and people of the said kingdom ... to be for ever absolved from ... all manner of duty of dominion, allegiance and obedience.

The Gunpowder Plot

The most famous crime committed by Catholics for their religion was the Gunpowder Plot of 1605 (see also the Case File, pp. 58–9). When Elizabeth was succeeded by the Stuart James I in 1603, English Catholics hoped that their sufferings might come to an end. As he was the son of Mary, Queen of Scots, Catholics hoped he might have some sympathy for his mother's friends. James did suspend the recusancy laws, which forced people to attend attend church, but reimposed them under pressure from public opinion.

Disappointed, a group of Catholics decided instead to destroy the government by blowing up the Houses of Parliament when the King was there. Accordingly, they hired a cellar below the parliament building, and an Anglo-Spanish adventurer named Guido Fawkes, to carry out the task. But one of the plotters wrote to warn a relative, Lord Monteagle, to stay away from the State opening of parliament, and Monteagle showed the letter to the Secretary of State, Robert Cecil. Cecil ordered a search of parliament and found the store of gunpowder in the cellars as Guy Fawkes was preparing it. Fawkes was tortured in the Tower of London and revealed the names of his fellow conspirators. They were hunted down, captured and executed as traitors. Guy Fawkes himself was hanged, drawn and quartered while the citizens of London celebrated his failure by burning his effigy on street bonfires.

The later Stuarts and after

Religion and the organisation of the Church were important factors contributing to the Civil Wars of the 1640s and the Revolution of 1688. Both Charles I (1625–49) and James II (1685–8) were accused of having Catholic views, and in 1689 the Bill of Rights laid down that no Catholic could reign in Britain. To protect this settlement, the English imposed it on Ireland and Scotland. The Test Acts of 1673 and 1678 banned Catholics from the universities, from government office and from sitting in parliament.

Persecution began to die down in England from 1689 on, when William III and Mary II became king and queen, although anti-Catholic prejudice could still lead to disorder. In 1780, for example, Lord George Gordon stirred up the London mob to terrorise the capital for three days in protest against the Catholic Relief Act.

Questions

1 Why was it so difficult to bring religious divisions to an end in Tudor and Stuart England?

2 How far was it a crime to be a Catholic?

The Gunpowder Plot

▶ **Who was really responsible for the plot?**

Source A
An engraving
made in 1606
of the execution
of the plotters

Some historians have argued that the Gunpowder Plot of 1605 was known to the authorities, and possibly even invented by them, to discredit Catholics and smoke out possible disloyalty. It has been suggested that the plotters were tricked into taking part. Sources **B** to **I** explore all these theories and discuss the effects of the plot.

Source B   Details of the plot

Robert Catesby, Thomas Winter, Thomas Percy, John Wright and Guy Fawkes plotted to blow up King James I when he opened Parliament on 5 November 1605. A wealthy Catholic called Francis Tresham agreed to provide money and soldiers to help them seize control when the king was dead ... The new cellar went under the House of Lords itself. The plotters stored 16 barrels of gunpowder there and made their final plans. But on 26 October 1605 a mysterious stranger delivered an unsigned letter to Lord Monteagle, a Catholic, just as he was having dinner at home. Monteagle had been involved in an earlier plot with Catesby and Tresham (his wife's brother).

   Lord Monteagle took the letter at once to the king's chief minister, Robert Cecil, Earl of Salisbury. On 4 November Cecil sent soldiers to search the cellars. Just before midnight they found the gunpowder hidden behind a stack of firewood. They also found a man with matches, fuse and lantern.... It was Guido (Guy) Fawkes. The other plotters fled. Catesby and Percy were shot resisting arrest and all except Tresham (who died of a mysterious illness) were executed.

From P. Sauvain, *Changing World*, 1992

Source C   From Guy Fawkes' confession, 17 November 1605

Thomas Percy hired a house at Westminster near the Parliament House, and we began to make a mine [tunnel]. About Candlemas [2 February] 1605, we were half[way] through. We heard in the cellar next door the removing of coals. Finding this cellar was to be let, Percy went and hired it. We had before this brought into the house twenty barrels of powder, which we removed into the cellar, and covered with firewood.

Source D   Catholics look for 'a sudden blow'

Although most English Catholics were loyal to the crown and the Pope, the religious struggles of the sixteenth century had been fought out in an international context, and a few conspirators looked abroad for aid in restoring Catholicism to England. Frustrated at James' peaceful succession some had engaged in the half-baked Main and Bye Plots; these had little effect other than shocking the tolerant James into agreeing to new sanctions [laws] against recusants – the spring of 1605 brought over 5000 convictions and fines. But the peace with Spain [1604] came as a greater disappointment to those who had looked to Spain for help and they turned their thoughts to a 'sudden blow'. The opening of the new session of parliament in November 1605 seemed their chance to destroy the whole persecuting elite as well as the protestant king.

Adapted from D. Hirst, *Authority and Conflict*, 1986

Source E   The causes and effects of the plot

James' tactic of buying time by promising all things to all men misfired badly with the Roman Catholics, who believed the King's vague promises of toleration, and were disappointed when he bowed to pressure for persecution. The result was a stop-go policy on the enforcement of the penal laws which enraged the extreme Catholics and brought on the Gunpowder Plot of 1605. The whole wretched affair weakened the long-term prospects of Catholicism; the annual church service commemorating it continued well into Queen Victoria's reign, and it was still being thrown in the faces of the English Catholics under Edward VII in the early 1900s. But in the short term the repercussions were surprisingly mild; Parliament put another two penal laws on the statute book in 1606 and a third in 1610.

Adapted from J.P. Kenyon, *Stuart England*, 1978

Source F The plotters, drawn by Simon Pass in 1606

Source I The letter delivered to Lord Monteagle. The first four lines of the letter read: 'My Lord, out of the love I bear to some of your friends, I have a care of your preservation. Therefore I would advise you as you tender [care for] your life to devise some excuse to shift off [get out of] your attendance at this parliament.'

Source G Persecution and national unity

The Plot caused a new outbust of persecution. New sanctions enacted in 1606 made life more uncomfortable for the propertied, who could be blackmailed by informers or who attracted the attentions of needy courtiers. The most immediate result of the plot was, however, a strengthening of national unity. Despite the peace with Spain, the king could still be portrayed as leading the godly against a satanic popish foe. Anti-Catholicism entered the fabric of national life. In 1606 the outburst of patriotic fervour far outweighed resentment of James' extravagant spending, and resulted in a grant of money [from parliament].

Adapted from D. Hirst, *Authority and Conflict*, 1986

Source H The plot was not an invention

Salisbury's attempt to implicate the Society of Jesus [Jesuits] in the plot have roused suspicions that the whole affair was invented by the government. This is to attribute to seventeenth-century governments a degree of intelligence and authority only displayed (and that rarely) by all-powerful modern agencies like the KGB and CIA. The conspirators' leaders had already been implicated in the very Protestant rising of the Earl of Essex in 1601, and some historians see them not as religious fanatics at all, but poor gentry who found release for their economic and social grievances in Catholic activism; 'Robin Hoods', Salisbury called them, with a flick of contempt.

Adapted from J.P. Kenyon, *Stuart England*, 1978

Questions

1 Read Sources **B** and **C**. Do any parts of the account of events seem unlikely to have happened that way, or raise doubts about whether the plot was genuine? If you were able to cross-examine those involved, what questions would you like to ask them?

2 Examine Source **F**. How does it portray the plotters?

3 Sources **C** and **F** are contemporary sources. How far would you consider them to be reliable evidence?

4 Source **I** is a copy of the actual letter sent to Monteagle. How would you explain its untidy appearance and presentation? Read as much of it as you can. Does it seem to be the work of a wealthy and educated man? (Give reasons for your answer.)

5 Using the information in Sources **B**, **C** and **F**, who might have sent the letter? Why do you think Monteagle took the letter to Robert Cecil?

6 What motives for the plot are suggested in Sources **D** and **E**?

7 In what ways do Sources **E** and **G** suggest that the government gained from the plot? Does this mean that the government had a motive to arrange the plot? And if so, does this mean that it *did* arrange the plot?

Crime and superstition: witches and witchcraft

▶ *Why did people believe in witches? Why did the witchcraft scare happen?*

The witchcraft scare

The rise and decline of religious persecution was accompanied by a similar and related development – the witchcraft scare. Witchcraft had always been a crime, but until the sixteenth century it was treated as a minor crime and usually dealt with in the church courts (see Source **A**). In 1542, however, Henry VIII passed an Act of Parliament which made it a felony, punishable by death. In 1563 a further Act listed different kinds of witchcraft, and in 1604 all the earlier laws were brought together.

The attention given to witchcraft in parliament reflected what was happening in the country at large. The sixteenth century saw a massive rise in accusations of witchcraft, and in the harsh treatment of witches (see Source **B**). Prosecutions reached a peak in Elizabeth's reign, and again during the Civil War of the 1640s (see Source **C**). Witch hunts were common, and often hysterical, making it impossible for the accused to receive any justice.

Source A   Why people consulted witches

For generations people had been turning to 'cunning men' and 'wise women', 'sorcerers', 'conjurors', 'blessers' and 'charmers' for protection against pain and illness and early death, and against fire and dearth [scarcity], for magical cures and love potions, for help in the recovery of stolen goods or the discovery of buried treasure or missing children. The witches consulted offered all manner of treatment and wizardries, from curing headaches by boiling a lock of the patient's hair in urine, then throwing it into the fire, to treating sick animals by tapping them with magic wands or tying bunches of herbs to their tails ... yet it seems that before 1500 it was extremely rare for witches to suffer more than the mildest punishments; and ... examination of medieval judicial records has so far revealed no more than a dozen known cases of supposed witches being executed for the whole period between the Norman conquest and the Reformation. And most of these had been involved in plots against the monarch or his friends.

From C. Hibbert, *The English*, 1994

Source B   The prosecution of witches in Elizabeth's reign

Lesser forms of witchcraft were regularly presented before the Elizabethan ecclesiastical courts ... As Elizabeth's reign progressed, witchcraft in Yorkshire began to figure among the concerns of the secular [non-religious] authorities. In 1583, three women ... were pilloried in Hull. In 1597 the Privy Council issued a pardon to Elizabeth Melton of Collingham who had been convicted for witchcraft. In 1603 a woman named Mary Panell, whose reputation for witchcraft stretched back at least to bewitching a man to death in 1593, was executed at Ledston. In 1604, again at Hull, four witches (three women and one man) were executed, one of them 'confessing many things and at his death accusing divers [various others] for witchcraft' ... The thickening of such references around the beginning of the seventeenth century suggests a growing awareness of witchcraft as a problem.

From J.A. Sharpe, *Witchcraft in Seventeenth Century Yorkshire*, 1992

Source C   The prosecution of witches reaches its height

Towards the middle of the seventeenth century ... witch-hunts became much more hysterical than they had in the past; and, although many judges lamented the vindictiveness with which they were pursued – and some, like Lord Chief Justice, Sir John Holt, who seemed 'to believe nothing of witchery at all', did their best to bring about acquittals – there were others who seemed determined to secure conviction even on the flimsiest of evidence. Lord Chief Justice North confessed that he had condoned [allowed] the conviction of three innocent women at Exeter because he feared that acquittal might result in a fresh wave of witch-hunting.

From C. Hibbert, *The English*, 1994

Margaret Harkett was a sixty-year-old widow from Stanmore in Middlesex. She was caught picking peas in a neighbour's field without permission. When the neighbour asked her to give back the peas, she became angry and threw them down on the ground. From that time, no peas would grow in the field. A bailiff found her taking wood from his master's land. He hit her, and later he went mad. A neighbour bought a pair of shoes from Margaret, but he did not give enough money. He later died. In 1585 Margaret Harkett was executed in London as a witch.

Jane Kighly came into the house of Abraham Hobson in Idle in 1649, stroked a pig that was standing by the fire, and said that it would go mad, which it promptly did, dying half an hour later. Hobson also claimed that a fortnight after the previous Christmas he had attended a 'pig feast' where he met Kighly, who told him 'she loved him and all his house' and gave him 'a little clap on his knee'. The next day his knee swelled up, and eventually became paralysed.

Margaret Flower was a servant to Francis Manners, Earl of Rutland; her mother (Joan) and sister were also employed there. When Margaret was dismissed for stealing in 1612, the Earl and his family fell ill, and one of his sons died. The three women were accused of witchcraft. Joan Flower angrily denied it, saying that she hoped the bread and butter that she had just eaten would choke her if she were guilty. At that, she dropped down dead. Margaret and her sister were tried for witchcraft and hanged.

The causes of the witchcraft scare

Historians have argued that a number of factors combined to bring about this new attention to witchcraft, and the new severity in dealing with it. The Reformation caused political divisions over religion, and encouraged the government to enquire more carefully into people's beliefs and activities; and because witchcraft was secretive, it was bound to arouse suspicion. Protestant ideas made much of the danger of sin, and the lurking threat of the devil, who tried to tempt souls into black religion and magic. Puritans tended to regard the Catholic Church as the creation of the devil, and the Pope as Anti-Christ, while the Catholic Church increasingly regarded Protestant heretics in the same way. Such a climate of belief, and the general intensity aroused by religious issues in this period, was bound to make people more ready to believe that the devil was active in society, and to see those who claimed 'cunning' powers as evil rather than eccentric.

These conditions combined with social and economic changes to make the poor vulnerable and the rich wary. The growth of trade and changes in agriculture undermined village communities, allowing some people to increase in wealth and become prosperous yeomen, while others sank into wage labour or unemployment. Jealousy and fear were likely to encourage the kind of neighbour quarrels that often preceded accusations of witchcraft, and the kind of threats that some so-called witches uttered. In this context, the odd or the unusual, whether events or people, could easily seem sinister (See Source **D**). And once the scare had begun, and rumours of witchcraft increased, so the fear, and the 'evidence' that it was based on, could become more common and more easily believed.

The most vulnerable group were elderly women, who found it difficult to secure employment, and had little power to defend their interests. The Church had always taught that women were morally weaker than men, and more likely to do the devil's work, just as Eve had tempted Adam. Many old women lived alone, and often had pets for company, who could be considered their 'familiars' (spirits sent by the devil; see Source **E**). Over 90 per cent of witchcraft accusations in Essex involved old women who lived alone.

Source D John Gaule, a Huntingdonshire clergyman in the seventeenth century, protests at the witch scare

Every old woman with a wrinkled face, a furr'd brow, a hairy lip, a gobber tooth, a squint eye, a squeaking voice or a scolding tongue, having a ragged coat on her back, a skull-cap on her head, a spindle in her hand and a dog or cat by her side, is not only suspected but pronounced for a witch.

Source E A contemporary woodcut of a witch and her familiars

The most numerous and hysterical prosecutions seem to have occurred between 1645 and 1647, towards the end of the Civil War. Although the war and the upheaval involved may well have contributed to this, the main reason seems to have been the influence of a particular individual, Matthew Hopkins, who called himself the Witchfinder General. The son of a minister in Wenham, Suffolk, he seems to have first become acquainted with witches as a lawyer in Manningtree, where he secured the conviction of twenty-nine women in 1644. This seems to have convinced him that this was where his career lay, and he began to travel the country in search of witches.

His methods were cruel: they involved having women stripped, searched, bound and imprisoned in conditions of great discomfort, and being deprived of rest and sleep. Not surprisingly, many confessed, and Hopkins secured many convictions across the south-eastern counties of England. While not particularly religious, he does seem to have believed in his work. There is no evidence that he tried to make money, although he may well have found his fame, and his ability to terrorise the population, rewarding. After the publication of a book by John Gaule protesting at his activities (see Source **D**), Hopkins was himself accused of witchcraft, and forced to undergo the same treatment as his victims. He was hanged in August 1647.

The end of the scare

After the death of Matthew Hopkins (see box), trials and executions of witches became less frequent. An end to the upheaval and religious extremism of the Civil Wars, and the slowing in the pace of social and economic change, led to a more stable society. It was also a more rational society, aware of scientific thinking, and therefore less inclined to believe the charges of witchcraft. As with many crimes, evidence was being scrutinised more carefully, and sceptics were more able to speak out. In 1716 a man who accused a woman of bewitching him was eventually convicted at Surrey Assizes as a cheat and imposter. In 1736 the witchcraft laws were repealed, although public opinion took more convincing. Ducking of witches continued until at least 1751, and it is difficult to assess how many supposed witches received some kind of unofficial 'justice' in the more remote villages.

*Q*uestions

1 How does Source **A** portray witches as a useful part of country life?

2 What reasons can you give for a change in this attitude in the sixteenth and seventeenth centuries?

3 Which of these reasons are illustrated in the cases of the three witches (see box on p. 61)?

4 Sources **B** and **C** show how prosecutions increased. Why did this increase continue for so long?

5 Why were elderly women so often accused of being witches?

6 Look at Sources **C** and **D** and the information on Matthew Hopkins. Why was it so difficult to resist the witchcraft scare?

7 Using all the information that you have, explain why the witchcraft scare occurred in the later sixteenth and seventeenth centuries.

The development of religious freedom

▶ *Why did religious persecution end?*

Protestant Dissent

The decline in accusations of witchcraft coincided with a more rational approach to religion in general, which allowed greater religious freedom to develop. This was partly the result of Protestant Dissent and of Separatist campaigns for freedom of worship. Most Puritans obeyed the law by attending church regularly and attempting to reform it from within, but a few could not remain in the Church and wanted to separate from it. In the 1630s there were increasing numbers of Separatists, and when the English Civil War broke out in 1642 they found they could preach openly, without the censorship imposed by the bishops. Their numbers increased and their views and claims became increasingly radical. In 1649 they helped to bring Charles I to trial and execution for treason, and set up a Commonwealth in place of the monarchy.

Most people found this behaviour terrifying. Groups like the Quakers behaved in a distinctive and unusual way. They refused to take off their hats to their 'betters' in society and even allowed women to preach. The governing classes felt that natural order and authority were being destroyed. In 1656 James Naylor, a Quaker, re-enacted Christ's entry into Jerusalem with his own followers at Bristol. He was accused of blasphemy, whipped, bored through the tongue and imprisoned (see Source **A**).

The Nonconformists

In 1660, with the restoration of the monarchy, new laws revived the power of the Church and punished anyone who tried to worship outside it. These laws, known as the Clarendon Code, set out strict rules for Church ministers to follow, as well as fines and imprisonment for anyone caught attending private religious meetings. Those who were unable to accept the ideas of the Church of England became known as Nonconformists, or Protestant Dissenters.

The Quakers suffered particularly badly because they were easily recognisable and because they were open to special abuse. As they believed that it was wrong to swear an oath, they could not take the Oath of Allegiance (to obey the king and the law), which was a crime under treason laws. Their enemies often accused them of something that they had not done, so that when they were in court they had to refuse to take the Oath of Allegiance. Many Quakers were kept in prison for years this way, without any crime being proved against them.

Source A   The punishment of James Naylor, 1656

The end of persecution

But fears of Catholic influence over the king grew stronger and public attitudes towards Protestant Dissenters changed. In some places persecution was half-hearted and the authorities protected meetings. In Hull, for example, there were two Puritan meetings which were rarely troubled, and when ordered to enforce the laws, some aldermen (civic officials) chose to resign rather than obey.

By 1687 it was clear that persecution of Protestants was unpopular, and the threat posed by a Catholic monarch, James II, led the Church to look for allies. In 1688 Protestant Dissenters supported the Church and parliament in driving James off the throne, and were rewarded in 1689 with a Toleration Act, allowing Protestant groups to worship outside the Church. Now it was not a crime to worship differently from the king, and new religious movements such as the Methodists emerged.

Questions

1 Why were Separatists treated as criminals in the seventeenth century? What methods were used to persecute them?

2 What factors encouraged the government to become more tolerant of different religious groups?

10 Crime and protest, 1500–1750

Riots and rebellions

 How did the government react to protest?

Riot and reaction

Religion was only one thing that caused people to protest against what they saw as injustice. This was also a time of economic hardship and social change, and there were riots against enclosure and high prices as well as protests sparked off by religious fears (see Source **A**). Such protests were often harshly dealt with by a nervous government (see Source **B**).

Source A Apprentice rioters outside Lambeth Palace, 1640

The rising of Prentises and Sea-men on South=wark side to assault the Arch-bishops of Canter=burys House at Lambeth.

Source B Apprentice riots in London, 1595, based on a contemporary report

June 13 – Many apprentices, short of food, who were paid only 3d. instead of 5d., stole butter in Southwark Market ... and were locked in the Counter Prison because they denounced the Lord Mayor.
June 27 – The apprentices who had stolen butter were whipped, pilloried and imprisoned.
June 29 – Unruly youths on Tower Hill attacked the watch of that ward, and were arrested by the Sheriffs.
July 24 – Five of the unruly youths arrested on June 29 were drawn from Newgate to Tower Hill, where they were hanged and bowelled as traitors.

Full-scale rebellion

There were a number of full-scale rebellions between 1500 and 1750 (see Source **C**). These rebellions were often led by the governing class, motivated by their own ambitions and rivalries, who exploited the economic and religious grievances of the people to gain support. For the most part protest was *against* change and in favour of protecting traditional systems. Protestors often appealed to the monarch. Where the monarch was threatened, the aim was to replace the person, not change the system.

The main exception to this was in the Civil War, when Puritan Separatists wanted religious toleration, and the Levellers wanted a democratic republic in place of King Charles I. However, it was the special conditions of Civil War that allowed these ideas to develop, and after the monarchy was restored in 1660, such ideas were driven underground.

How was protest treated?

Protest was often recognised as political crime, and sometimes treated differently from ordinary crime. If it involved violence, or seriously threatened the government, it could be very harshly punished – a lot depended on how secure the government felt. The apprentices in Source **B** were acting at a time when the government was worried about unrest, which is why they were dealt with so severely.

In major rebellions, such as the Pilgrimage of Grace in 1536, retribution was harsh, but it was usually directed at the leaders who were punished for treason. An exception was the Monmouth Rebellion of 1685, where the notorious Judge Jeffries hanged hundreds of ordinary labourers in the Bloody Assizes (see Source **D**). After this, however, there was a widespread public revulsion, and Jeffries was later arrested and himself executed.

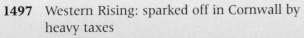

1497	Western Rising: sparked off in Cornwall by heavy taxes
1536	Pilgrimage of Grace: in northern England, protested against closure of monasteries; led by political faction of Catholic nobility
1549	Western Rising: wanted withdrawal of the new Prayer Book
1549	Kett's Rebellion: against enclosures and unemployment
1554	Wyatt's Rebellion: in Kent, against Mary's Spanish marriage and persecution of Protestants
1568	Northern Rising: led by northern Earls, who wanted to restore Catholicism, place Mary, Queen of Scots, on the throne, and regain their traditional power in northern England
1590s	Rebellion in Ireland: by Catholic earls against English control

1637	Scottish Rebellion: Scottish Covenanters rebel against the English Prayer Book being forced on the Scottish Church; religious and national grievances
1641	Irish Rebellion: against English power and the Protestant Church
1642–60	English Civil War and Interregnum
1685	Monmouth Rebellion: against James II and his Catholic policies
1688	Glorious Revolution: against James II and his Catholic policies
1690	Irish Rebellion: for James II and his Catholic policies
1715	Jacobite Rebellion: for James II and his Catholic policies
1745	Jacobite Rebellion: against union with England, for the return of the Stuart monarchy; led by the 'Young Pretender', Bonnie Prince Charlie

Major Holmes and 2 other Rebells Hanged in Chaines

Source D Rebels hanged after the Bloody Assizes, 1685

Sometimes protest could bring changes in the system, as the Protestant Dissenters showed. After 1688 religious toleration, economic prosperity and the possibility of working out political quarrels through parliament led to a reduction in serious rebellions, and protest was often treated more tolerantly (see p. 74).

Questions

1 What were the main sources of popular protest in this period?

2 Why did protesters often rely on upper-class leadership?

3 Why do you think the protesters in Sources **B** and **D** were so harshly treated?

4 Does Source **C** show any changes in the patterns and causes of protest between 1500 and 1750?

5 How would you use your knowledge of the period to explain these changes?

11 Crime and society in the eighteenth century

Law and property

▶ *Did the legal system provide justice?*

Improvements in law enforcement

By the mid-eighteenth century law enforcement had improved. Law textbooks were published, which helped less educated justices, as did the spread of literacy and the practice of the gentry sending their sons to the Inns of Court in London for basic legal education. Early legal text books by Marow (1503), Fitzherbert (1538) and Lambarde (1581) led finally to Richard Burn's four-volume collection, *The Justice of the Peace and the Parish Officer*, in 1754. More clergy were appointed as justices; they tended to be well educated, and brought with them the reforming purpose that had always existed within the church courts. Source **A** shows the increasing quality and confidence of many JPs by the middle of the century.

Source A JPs in the eighteenth century

▼

Eighteenth century JPs were increasingly willing to deal with minor crimes on the spot, and to investigate before allowing a case to proceed further. Wood theft, the embezzlement [theft] of materials by employees, game cases, vagrancy – all these were increasingly dealt with by justices sitting alone at home ... Even more striking ... by the middle years of the eighteenth century more and more magistrates were taking it upon themselves to throw out weak cases ... at the preliminary fact-gathering stage.

From J. Briggs et al., *Crime and Punishment in England*, 1996

Parish officials, aided by the system of poor relief, gave JPs a means of local supervision and support. The quality of these officials – parish constables, bailiffs and overseers of the poor – also benefited from the spread of education and the growth of a rural middle class of yeoman farmers.

In the larger towns and cities, where community structures were weaker, other improvements took place. From 1737 'rotation offices' were set up, in which JPs took turns to be on duty every day. The offices provided a small force of constables to catch criminals. They received a small salary, and a reward for each criminal they caught. There were also attempts to improve the quality of watchmen, and their job was made easier by the spread of street

The Fielding brothers

Henry Fielding was a barrister and author of the famous novel *Tom Jones*, before becoming the Bow Street Justice in 1748. He encouraged crimes to be reported and set up a group of six men, known as the Bow Street Runners, to pursue criminals. By 1754 he had done much to break up the notorious London gangs, when the work was taken over by his half-brother, Sir John. He in turn set up a national information network and encouraged JPs, mayors, innkeepers and others to report details of criminals and unsolved crimes. The information was then published in a broadsheet called *The Hue and Cry*. In 1763 he set up a highway patrol to combat highwaymen, and within a year the roads were clear. But the patrols were then disbanded and the highwaymen returned.

lighting – there were oil lamps in London by the 1680s, in Bristol and Norwich a decade later, and in Hull by 1713.

Court practice and new punishments

When cases did come to court, the accused benefited from a number of improvements that had taken place in the conduct of trials. The independence of juries was established by the Bushell case of 1671, when a jury refused to convict Protestant Dissenters on the judge's orders; and the independence of judges was established by the Act of Settlement in 1701. From 1702 witnesses had to give evidence on oath, and hearsay evidence was discouraged.

However, much still depended on the quality and availability of JPs. Punishment remained harsh, and the number of offences defined as felonies (punishable by death) mounted steadily. Death could be avoided by benefit of clergy and 'benefit of belly' (pregnancy), but the main alternative was transportation to North America, which began in 1678. In 1718 the Transportation Act extended and organised the process so that felons who were given benefit of clergy or pardoned by a judge were transported for seven or fourteen years, depending on the seriousness of the crime.

Socio-political crime

An increasing number of those who were hanged or transported were accused of a new range of crimes, called by historians 'Social' or 'socio-political' crime. By this they mean crimes which were defined as crimes by law, but seen by many as traditional, acceptable behaviour. For example, the protection of property and land became an increasing focus of the law, so that traditional habits such as the collection of wood and snaring animals for food, which was important for the poorer classes, became crimes (see Sources **B** and **C**).

Game laws were not enforced very strictly until the middle of the eighteenth century, when as they began to use guns, poachers were treated with far less leniency. An Act of 1770 made poachers liable to six months imprisonment; another of 1803 made them liable to hanging if they were armed and resisted arrest. By 1827 one seventh of all convicted criminals were poachers.

From C. Hibbert, *The English*, 1994

Source B Poaching and the game laws

In Windsor Forest and Waltham Chase, Hampshire, groups of men with blackened faces and calling themselves the Blacks broke into parks and forests, killed and carried off deer, attacked constables and threatened the farmers, gentry and their property. The Waltham Black Act, passed in 1723, introduced about fifty new capital offences related to poaching of fish and game, theft of trees and wood, and damage to property.

Smuggling

To protect Britain's growing trade, duties (taxes) were charged on imported goods, but this only raised the costs for those who could least afford it. By the mid-eighteenth century the crimes of wood theft, poaching, smuggling and wrecking were increasingly common, and were often harshly punished. Smuggling only really ended after 1840, when Sir Robert Peel reduced customs duties which meant that the risks were not worthwhile.

Smugglers were (and are) often misinterpreted as romantic adventurers, but the reality was often very different

(see Source **D**). The real image of smugglers may be seen in an incident in Dorset in 1748. The Hawkhurst Gang were chased and their cargo confiscated, but thirty smugglers broke into the Customs House at Poole and took it back. As they left, one of the smugglers gave a friend of his, Daniel Chater, a bag of tea. Later the authorities sent a Revenue officer, William Galley, to bring Chater to Chichester to give evidence. The smugglers seemed to have assumed that he was an informer, and when the pair stopped at the White Hart Inn in Rowland's Castle, they were waylaid. Half-drunk, they were taken out, whipped and dragged behind their horses. Both were mutilated, and then Galley was buried, probably while still alive. Chater was thrown down a dry well and stoned to death. A reward of 500 pounds was offered, and on this occasion the smugglers were arrested. Three were hanged, and the fourth died in prison.

Source D
Smugglers as adventurers

Smugglers were regarded as romantic adventurers performing a service used by all sensible people. Sir Robert Walpole, the king's chief minister, used an Admiralty barge to bring his smuggled wine up the Thames and was thought none the worse for that. A keg of contraband [smuggled] brandy was left at the door of the house on the Isle of Wight where the writer Elizabeth Sewell stayed, as a token of gratitude for the free passage that the smugglers enjoyed through the grounds.

From C. Hibbert, *The English*, 1994

Source C
A man-trap used to deter poaching

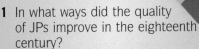

Questions

1 In what ways did the quality of JPs improve in the eighteenth century?

2 What other improvements were there in law enforcement in this period?

3 What was socio-political crime?

4 What sort of evidence would suggest that people of all classes were sympathetic to smuggling as a crime?

5 If smugglers were popular, why do you think the authorities were able to catch those who attacked Galley and Chater?

6 Why do you think poachers were more harshly treated than smugglers?

Overview

The effects of the Industrial Revolution

Between the mid-eighteenth century and the end of the Second World War, British society was transformed enormously by the effects of the Industrial Revolution. For the first time technology allowed production to increase without limit. Britain's population soared, as shown in Source **A**, and this population gradually shifted from the country into new towns.

Source A Graph showing population growth, 1701–1981

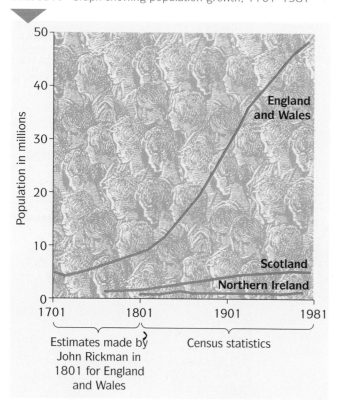

Estimates made by John Rickman in 1801 for England and Wales

Census statistics

By 1850 the urban population had overtaken country-dwellers, and more people were employed in industry than in agriculture (see Source **B**). Wealth increased hugely, at first for the middle and upper classes, but for the working classes too in the form of mass-produced goods which they could afford. Gradually, the government improved the living and working conditions of ordinary people, through education, laws and services. Most of the population were literate and aware of the wider world beyond Britain – the vast empire that she ruled.

Source B An observation made by William Cobbett on his rides around early nineteenth-century England

All the way along from Leeds to Sheffield it is coal and iron, and iron and coal. It was dark before we reached Sheffield, so that we saw the iron furnaces in all the horrible splendour of their everlasting blaze. Nothing can be conceived more grand or more terrific than the yellow waves of fire that incessantly issue from the tops of these furnaces.

Between 1750 and 1950, society in Britain had become richer, more orderly, more respectable and with more to lose from crime. This was not achieved easily and change brought new opportunities for crime. Industrial development saw rapid urban growth in which communities broke down, slum housing proliferated, and unemployment or under-employment was a problem. These processes are illustrated in Sources **B** to **D**.

Source C Diagram showing the changing balance of urban and rural population, 1800–1950

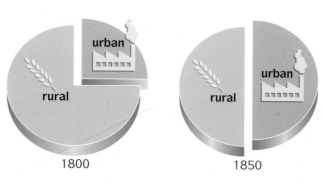

1800

1850

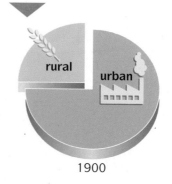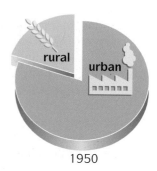

1900

1950

The problems of greater wealth

In these conditions crime increased and law enforcement deteriorated. Greater wealth meant more to steal and deprivation led to drunkenness, violence and brutality. A system of law enforcement that still relied on community effort and local knowledge inevitably struggled to cope; and harsh punishments were little deterrent as criminals knew they could usually escape capture or trial.

Government and 'respectable' society reacted by redefining crimes as felonies and increasing the harshness of the punishments. But by the 1830s this approach was clearly cruel, arbitrary and also largely ineffective. Gradually, attitudes towards criminals began to change. Reformers encouraged greater understanding of the causes of crime and tried to propose punishments that would help to reduce it. Large urban populations led to the development of working-class organisations able to protest for change. The result was a period of reform, and by the mid-nineteenth century the government had a range of resources and methods not seen since the Roman Empire.

The effects of reform

Money and power allowed central government to take on new responsibilities; new technology and communications allowed it to extend its authority nationwide; and political changes recognised the existence and rights of a respectable working class. The result was a public system of law enforcement. The government accepted a new responsibility for catching and prosecuting criminals rather than leaving it to the victim. This system was expected to be professional, adequately trained and adequately resourced. And while deterrence and retribution remained powerful influences, the possibilities of reform and rehabilitation, to bring criminals back into society, were increasingly considered. Between 1750 and 1950 new skills, new resources and the desire for improvement brought revolutionary changes in crime and in how it was treated.

Questions

1 What problems did the Industrial Revolution create?

2 What benefits did it bring?

3 Why did governments need to take on new responsibilities?

4 Why were they able to do so?

13 The need for reform, 1750–1820

Patterns of crime

▶ *Why did crime increase in the eighteenth and nineteenth centuries?*

Source A *Prison*: a scene from Hogarth's *The Rake's Progress* (c. 1733), a series of paintings which illustrate the decline and fall of a dissolute member of the upper classes

Source B A comment by Henry Fielding, in his *Inquiry into the Causes of the Late Increase of Robbers*, 1751

I think that the vast torrent of luxury which of late years hath poured itself into this nation hath greatly contributed to produce the mischief ... It reaches the very dregs of the people, who ... not being able by the fruits of honest labour to support the state which they [desire], they disdain the wages to which their industry would entitle them; the more simple and poor-spirited betake themselves to a state of starving and beggary, while those of more art and courage become thieves and robbers.

Throughout the eighteenth and early nineteenth centuries, contemporaries were convinced that crime was increasing, and complaints were numerous. In 1751 King George II expressed his concern about 'outrages and violences, which are inconsistent with all good government, and endanger the lives and properties of my subjects'. The growing wealth of eighteenth-century England had created corruption and encouraged greed at the top and crime at the bottom of society (see Sources **A** and **B**).

Careful study of available records has allowed the historian Clive Emsley to draw some general conclusions about patterns of crime. Before 1750 there is little evidence of any marked increase in crime, and after 1850 there seems to have been a decline in theft and violence. Between 1750 and 1850, however, there was a marked increase in crime, within which there were certain clear patterns:

- A gradual increase in theft and assault occurred during the second half of the eighteenth century.
- Murders and the threat of random violence created the greatest fears, but the vast majority were committed by persons well known to the victims; the most common crime was small-scale theft.

The committal statistics published by the government show an almost seven-fold increase between 1805 and 1842, with the highest figure, 31,309 committals, reached in that year. The increase in population was enormous during these years, but at about 80% it was well below the increase in crime. Moreover, the crime increase seems to have been as marked in predominantly rural counties, like Bedfordshire and Sussex, as it was overall. What is especially noticeable about the peaks of committals in the first half of the nineteenth century, is how they coincide with years marked by economic depression and political unrest. Crime appears to increase when there is concern about public disorder.

Other factors also influence the figures. Young men in their late teens were often employed as apprentices, poorly paid and dependent on employers; if they left their masters for any reason, they moved onto the margins of society. As craftsmen were overtaken by machines, artisans lost any protection against cheap labour. War brought a reduction in crime, perhaps because such surplus males were taken up by the armed forces – but peace brought an upsurge as they returned to the labour market. Around one quarter of a million men were demobilised onto a contracting labour market in 1814 and 1815.

Adapted from C. Emsley, Crime and Society in England, 1750-1900, 1987

Source C The increase in crime in the early nineteenth century

Source D Patterns of crime in early nineteenth-century England

Source E The case of William King and John Gascoigne who were committed in 1820 for the theft of fowls, ten bushels of soot and a bridle. Statements from the two men claimed poverty in mitigation.

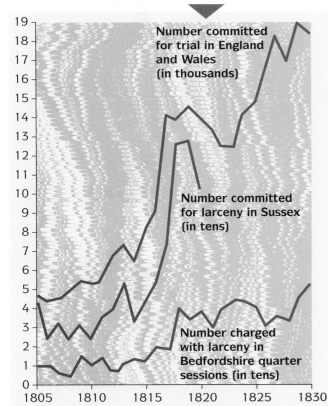

William King – 'I was in distress. I had neither money nor victuals [food], and was forced to do something. I was going about the country to look for work.'
John Gascoigne – 'I could get no work, nor any victuals, and was driven to it. We were to have 10 pence a bucket for the soot … and we roasted one of the fowls under a hedge.'

Source F The case of John Stone, who was prosecuted in 1822 for stealing a watch, an offence which could carry the death penalty.

'I am a poor stocking weaver in distress. I was travelling into Leicestershire, after having been to London to offer myself for a soldier; but was not tall enough. My parents are in distress, my father out of employment. I have eight brothers and sisters.'

- Most offenders, about three-quarters, were young men in their late teens and early twenties.
- Crime increased in times of economic difficulty and shortages, particularly among women and married men.
- Crime fell in times of war, only to rise rapidly when peace returned and soldiers were demobilised.

To investigate these patterns of crime, and suggest some reasons for them, you will need to interpret the sources in this unit in the context of the historical period. Sources **C** and **D** provide statistics and a summary of criminal behaviour; Sources **E** and **F** are examples of crimes.

uestions

1 What does Source **C** tell you about patterns of crime in this period?

2 How would you use the other sources and your knowledge to explain the fluctuations within the overall pattern?

3 Why would the growth of industry and towns make crime worse?

4 How do Sources **E** and **F** help to explain the increase in rural crime?

5 How would you explain the increase in crime in this period?

The Bloody Code

▶ *What was the reaction to the growth in crime?*

The causes of crime

It is clear that people did not know why crime was increasing in this period. Commentators such as Henry Fielding in the 1750s and Patrick Colquhoun in the 1790s identified a link between crime and poverty, as Source **A** shows (and see also p. 70). But their view was that people were poor and criminal because they were lazy and corrupt. Some commentators, however, were willing to blame the upper classes for setting a bad example, and for failing to provide good moral education and sound discipline.

Source A In his *Treatise on the Police of the Metropolis*, 1795, Patrick Colquhoun sees the poor as responsible for their own distress

▼

Were we to examine the history of any given number of these our miserable fellow-mortals, it would be discovered that their distress, almost in every instance, has been occasioned by extravagance, idleness, profligacy, and crimes: and that their chief support is by gambling, cheating and thieving in a little way.

Nevertheless, they were sure that crime was carried out by the working classes. They admitted that some poor people were respectable, but on the whole the poor had the potential for crime. It is not surprising that the government response to the problems of crime was one of repression. Only the most enlightened argued for education, discipline and the establishment of an effective police force. While parliamentary reports considered ways of policing, the government relied on deterrence through ever harsher punishment, and the development of the Bloody Code.

The Bloody Code

The Bloody Code is the term used by nineteenth-century reformers to describe this penal system. The death penalty was at the centre of the system and the number of crimes punishable by death increased in this period. In 1603 only fifty crimes were classified as capital offences (those punishable by death). By 1815 the figure was more than two hundred. Stealing property worth a shilling, setting fire to a heap of hay or defacing Westminster Bridge were all, in theory, hanging offences. Sources **B** to **H** provide more details.

Source B The number of capital offences

▼

An extraordinary number of crimes were punishable by death. According to Sir Thomas Fowell Buxton in the early nineteenth century, there were as many as 223 of them, four made capital by the Plantagenets, 26 by the Tudors, 36 in the time of the Stuarts and no less than 156 since. Apart from such crimes as treason, murder, piracy, arson, stealing, rape, sodomy and various breaches of the game laws … it was an offence punishable by death to impersonate a Chelsea Pensioner, to make a false entry in the books of the Bank of England, to strike a Privy Councillor or to refuse to remain in quarantine.

Adapted from C. Hibbert, *The English*, 1994

Source C How the offences were defined

▼

One of the key errors of many historians … has been to take the eighteenth-century 'Bloody Code' at a face value based on modern perceptions of the law; thus they have assumed that the increase in capital statutes in the eighteenth century was a meaningful one. In reality, offences were defined in a very narrow way … Destroying Westminster Bridge was the same kind of offence as destroying Fulham Bridge, but each offence had its own capital statute. According to Peel in 1826, there were twenty statutes concerning the protection of trees from theft and wilful damage.

From C. Emsley, *Crime and Society in England, 1750–1900*, 1987

Source D Executions of the young

If executions were declining, they were still common enough. A witness said that he had twice seen forty men hanged in a single day; and out of every twenty criminals hanged, so it was estimated, eighteen were less than twenty-one years old. Many were under fifteen. In 1801 a boy aged thirteen was sentenced to death for breaking into a house and stealing a spoon; two sisters aged eight and eleven were similarly sentenced at Lynn in 1808.

From C. Hibbert, *The English*, 1994

Source E An extract from Henry Fielding's novel *Joseph Andrews*, 1742

The Squire asked for what crimes the couple had been committed. 'No great crime' answered the Justice, 'I have only ordered them to Bridewell for month.' 'But what is their crime?' repeated the Squire. 'Larceny [theft] an't please your Honour,' said Scout. 'Aye' said the Justice, 'a kind of felonious, larcenous thing. I believe I must order them a little correction too, a little stripping and whipping.' When pressed further, the Justice revealed that, in walking through a field, the young man had cut a twig, worth 3p, which the young woman had received. 'Jesu!' said the Squire, 'would you commit two persons to Bridewell for a twig?' 'Yes' said the Lawyer, 'and with great lenity too; for if we had called it a young tree, they would both have been hanged.'

Source F Vengeance was not the purpose

In London and Middlesex between 1749 and 1799 ... at least half of those convicted of capital crimes were reprieved ... The pattern is very erratic: 90% of those convicted in 1752 – the year following Fielding's influential tract – were hanged, and 81% in 1787 ... In contrast, only one in ten of those capitally convicted in 1794, and one in eight in 1797, were executed. This was not merely the tempering with mercy of a brutal penal code. The word to keep in mind is not 'mercy' but 'discretion'. The landed rulers of England did not need to hang all those convicted of felony; the purpose was example, not vengeance.

From J. Rule, *Albion's People*, 1992

Source G A decline in the number of hangings

The eighteenth century saw a growing gap between those convicted of capital crimes and those actually hanged. Those convicted of theft were most likely to be reprieved, those using violence in some form were usually executed. Of the 97 hanged in London and Middlesex in 1785, only one was a murderer but 43 had been convicted of burglary and house-breaking, and 31 of highway robbery. What enabled so many minor criminals to escape death was the development of transportation. Transportation allowed the authorities to continue limiting actual deaths to what was required for the purposes of example.

Adapted from J. Rule, *Albion's People*, 1992

Source H There were many complaints that public hangings did not make an example of the criminal but were public holidays. This illustration by Hogarth shows the fairground atmosphere that often prevailed.

Questions

1 Read Sources **B** to **E**. What evidence suggests that the treatment of criminals under the Bloody Code was brutal?

2 What does Source **F** suggest about the aims of punishment in this period?

3 What do Sources **F** and **G** tell us about how the laws were applied in practice?

4 Does Source **H** prove that public hangings were not a deterrent?

5 Source **E** comes from a novel. Does this make it unreliable as evidence?

6 By the early 1800s some MPs favoured reform of the laws. Use the evidence here in the context of the period to compose a letter to *The Times* supporting calls for reform.

 How did the government react to protest?

Riots and the lower classes

A further illustration of the growing concern with crime in this period is the way in which popular protests were treated. In the sixteenth and seventeenth centuries, a time of hardship and unrest, protest was often harshly punished. By the eighteenth century the nature and treatment of popular protest changed. Political battles involving the ruling class were now solved through party rivalry in parliament. Popular protest through rioting became more strictly confined to the lower classes. It rarely threatened government and so was treated with some tolerance.

Rioters often acted against particular targets, for example merchants accused of hoarding food and charging high prices. Once the rioters had seized the food, however, they often insisted on paying what they considered to be a fair price. As Source **A** indicates, sometimes rioting was accepted as the only way in which ordinary people could express their views.

Source A The causes of the disturbances

The most common causes of disturbances were food shortages, recruiting (for the army), enclosures and turnpikes. Rioters were the urban poor and, in most cases, disturbances were surprisingly orderly. In some areas the local authorities were in sympathy with the rioters. Ordinary people were not opposed to enclosures in principle, but took action when they felt a sense of injustice at the loss of customary common grazing rights. Turnpike roads, with their frequent toll-gates, were resented as an indirect form of taxation. Anti-turnpike disturbances, which usually amounted to the destruction of turnpike-houses and toll-gates, were infrequent in comparison to the number of roads built.

Adapted from R. Ellis, *People, Power and Politics*, vol. 2, 1995

Source B The Gordon Riots, 1780

A hardening of attitudes

Although the government was able to treat most outbursts of popular resentment with some tolerance, this should not be exaggerated. The Riot Act of 1715 allowed troops to be used when the Act had been read, as a warning to the crowd to disperse. When things got out of hand the authorities could react strongly. In 1761 an anti-recruiting riot in Northumberland led to a crowd of 5,000 being fired on by the Yorkshire militia, causing about a hundred casualties, half of them fatal.

By the end of the eighteenth century, government attitudes and responses had hardened. This was due to growing unrest. Industrial development in the 1770s and 1780s threatened the livelihood of cloth-workers and led to outbreaks of machine breaking. Source **B** shows the Gordon Riots of 1780, sparked off by an attempt to extend the political rights of Roman Catholics, which resulted in week-long riot, eventually put down with almost 300 deaths by calling in 10,000 troops. Before that, however, the troops had roamed London aimlessly for lack of JPs able to direct and command them, demonstrating the inadequacy of the existing system of law enforcement.

Political unrest

For the government the situation became more serious after the revolution in France in 1789. The American War of Independence had already increased talk of democracy and the need for parliamentary reform, and the declarations of the French National Assembly and the execution of the French king in 1793 raised similar possibilities in Britain. Government fears were revealed by the treatment of Kid Wake and the members of the LCS – the London Corresponding Society (see Sources **C** and **D**). Although neither was a real threat, both were treated as a danger to the government itself.

Unrest was now often political: the aim of demonstrators was therefore regarded as the removal of the government itself. In October 1794 an LCS demonstration in Copenhagen Fields on the outskirts of London drew 100,000 people. Parliament passed an Act against Treasonable Practices which made it a crime to demand constitutional reform, and an Act against Seditious Meetings which made gatherings of more than fifty people illegal without permission from a JP. Two days later 200,000 supporters of reform gathered at Copenhagen Fields in defiance of the Act, leaving the government powerless.

The effects of further Acts, such as the Incitement of Mutiny Act in 1798 and the Combination Acts of 1800 which outlawed all political societies, dampened down protest movements. But the problems behind popular unrest had still not been addressed.

Source C Kid Wake in Gloucester Prison. Kid Wake was a London printer who was arrested in 1794 for shouting a protest against the French war as King George III was travelling to the opening of parliament. His shout of 'No George, no war' was treated as sedition and he was sentenced to five years in prison, isolated from other prisoners.

Source D Commemorative token celebrating the acquittal of the leaders of the London Corresponding Society. The society campaigned for reform of parliament. Although completely peaceful, its large-scale demonstrations frightened the government, and in 1794 the leaders were arrested and charged with treason. The jury refused to convict them on the basis that they had done nothing treasonable.

The Luddites

Some protesters focused on more practical matters and used direct action. The most famous outburst of machine-breaking came between 1811 and 1816, in what became known as the Luddite movement. Probably named after Ned Ludlam, the Luddites organised attacks on mills and factories throughout the Midlands and North. As local constables and JPs were unable to cope, factory owners recruited volunteers, and called on the government to send troops. At Rawfolds Mill, west Yorkshire, two Luddites were killed and a local mill-owner murdered; three Luddites were hanged for murder, and fourteen others for rioting. These problems showed how inadequate law enforcement still was, which led to new calls for a professional police force.

Questions

1 What were the causes of rioting in the eighteenth century?

2 Why did the government feel able to show some tolerance?

3 What evidence suggests that the government's attitude changed?

4 How was the government's attitude affected by:
a) the French Revolution;
b) changes in the nature of protest?

The Peterloo Massacre, 1819

▶ *Why did the massacre take place?*

Source A A meeting in the White Horse at Pentrich, possibly including the agent Oliver

By 1819 the government was very nervous about the possibility of a revolution similar to the one in France. The activities of the Luddites were followed by attempted risings in Pentrich in Derbyshire and the so-called March of the Blanketeers, both in 1817. In fact, both had been set up by the government agent Oliver, who acted as a spy to root out agitators, but who actually set up these plots in order to report them and justify his pay (see Source **A**).

At the same time, a movement for political reform had developed, which aimed at changing the way in which MPs were elected. Leaders such as Francis Place and Henry Hunt told working people that the best chance of improving their conditions was to win the vote. If working people could elect MPs they could influence them to deal with the problems of the working classes. Place and Hunt began to hold a series of peaceful meetings and demonstrations, both to spread their ideas and to show the government the extent of their support. It was at one of these meetings in 1819 that the Peterloo Massacre took place.

Sources **B** to **G** show what happened at Peterloo. Read them and interpret them in the context of the problems facing the government at the time, to decide exactly what happened and why such an incident took place.

Source B What happened at St Peter's Fields

▼

St Peter's Fields, Manchester was the setting for a meeting of 60,000 people campaigning for Manchester to be given MPs. The JPs could not believe that such a meeting would be peaceful, and had the volunteer yeomanry and regular troops standing by. When the meeting opened, they read the Riot Act and ordered the crowd to disperse. The Manchester Yeomanry Cavalry tried to arrest the speaker, Henry Hunt, but, untrained in crowd control, they charged into the crowd. The regular troops had to be sent in to beat back the crowd with the flat of their sabres to rescue the yeomanry. Between eleven and fifteen people were killed and over four hundred injured, a hundred of them women.

Adapted from R. Whiting, *Crime and Punishment*, 1986

Source C An eyewitness report from *Historical Sketches and Personal Recollections*, by J. Prentice, a working man who attended the meeting at St Peter's Fields

▼

I saw the main body proceeding towards St Peter's Fields, and never was a gayer spectacle ... The 'marching order', of which so much was said afterwards, was what we often see in the processions of Sunday school children ...Our company laughed at the fears of the Magistrates, and the remark was, that if the men intended mischief they would not have brought their wives, sisters, or children with them.

Source D   From the report sent by the Manchester magistrates to Lord Sidmouth, the Home Secretary, on the evening after the massacre

We did not see any guns or swords but there were plenty of sticks. Long before Mr Hunt arrived, we decided that the size and noisy behaviour of the crowd was enough to frighten and terrify all the King's subjects. We did not think that such a gathering could be justified for any reason. While the cavalry was getting ready to move in, they were jeered and shouted at by the crowd.

Source E   From the report of the Manchester magistrates to Lord Sidmouth on 1 July 1819 (six weeks before the meeting at St Peter's Fields)

We are convinced that a rising against the government has been planned. So far the working people have been very calm but we do not expect this to continue. The people's feelings are being stirred up by radicals at the meetings that are held nearly every week. We cannot prevent these meetings so we do not know how to stop the dangerous ideas of the radicals being spread among the people.

MANCHESTER HEROES

Source F   'Manchester Heroes' – a cartoon published in a radical newspaper of 1819

Source G   From an editorial in *The Times* newspaper, based on the report of John Tyas, who was on the platform at St Peter's Fields. He was not a radical or a friend of Mr Hunt.

In the middle of the chairman's speech, less than twenty minutes after the meeting started, the cavalry charged into the crowd, sword in hand, cut their way to the platform and arrested Mr Hunt and others. As the cavalry moved towards the platform some people threw stones and other objects at them but they soon turned and fled as the cavalry trampled down and cut down a number of people. Many of the crowd were women. About 8 or 10 people were killed and more than 100 were wounded, some seriously, some less so.

Was the meeting at Manchester unlawful? We believe not. Was the subject being discussed [a reform of parliament] an unlawful subject? Certainly not. Was anything done at the meeting BEFORE THE CAVALRY RODE IN against the law? According to our information the law was not broken in any way.

Questions

1   Source **A** illustrates the kind of activities the government had to deal with in the years before 1819. How does this help to explain why the cavalry were sent in at Peterloo?

2   What evidence shows that the meeting at Peterloo was intended to be peaceful?

3   What reasons did the magistrates give for ordering in the cavalry?

4   Using Sources **D** and **E** together, how far was the decision to send in the cavalry justified?

5   How far do Sources **F** and **G** agree? Which do you consider to be more useful?

6   Use the sources, interpreted in the context of your wider knowledge, to explain what happened at Peterloo and why it was important.

14 An age of reform, 1820–1950

The coming of reform

 How did law enforcement change in the nineteenth century?

The reformers: Jeremy Bentham

The Peterloo Massacre was followed by further repression in the 'Gag Acts' of 1819, which limited the right of reformers to meet or publish their ideas. It also led to public debate about the need for reform. Popular unrest and rising crime added weight to the arguments of reformers such as Sir Samuel Romilly, that the laws were too harsh and did not discriminate between different levels of crime. He eventually persuaded parliament to abolish the death sentence for pickpockets and some types of begging.

Others, such as the philosopher Jeremy Bentham, emphasised the inefficiency rather than the cruelty of relying on harsh punishment. Bentham's ideas were known as Utilitarianism; he argued that government should use people's natural talents to make arrangements that would work in the most practical way. This argument had a wide appeal and Bentham became very influential. Practical, enforceable laws were passed, and greater emphasis was placed on detecting and preventing crime, as well as reforming criminals into useful citizens.

Sir Robert Peel

One man influenced by Bentham's ideas was Sir Robert Peel, who became Home Secretary in 1822 (see Source **A**). Peel set about establishing a more rational system of law enforcement. His 1823 Gaols Act set standards of health and hygiene in gaols, replaced gaolers' fees with proper salaries, set rules for discipline and separated prisoners according to age and sex. He also reformed the law, reducing 300 criminal laws to four comprehensive ones, and reducing eight Acts on recruiting juries and 92 Acts on theft to one each. Judges could now impose reduced sentences for crimes that did not involve killing.

There had also been a growing demand for effective policing for some time. The existing Bow Street Runners in London had proved their value, as Source **B** shows, but the problems of crime in London revealed their limitations. Parliament was reluctant to act because of fears that the police would infringe people's liberties (see Source **C**). However, growing crime made some change necessary, and in 1829 Peel persuaded parliament to pass the Metropolitan Police Act, establishing a professional police force (the 'Peelers') in London. After they had shown their value, in 1835 the Municipal Corporation Act recommended borough councils to establish forces along the lines of the Metropolitan Police Force.

Source A Born in 1788, the son of a factory-owner, Sir Robert Peel later became Prime Minister. He reduced customs duties and made smuggling virtually unknown by the mid-1840s.

Source C From a parliamentary committee report, 1818

A continental police force would be odious and repulsive and make every servant of every house a spy on the actions of his master and all classes of society spy on each other.

As Source **D** shows, nineteenth-century governments created a better system of law enforcement. They covered three aspects of the system – the work of police in preventing and detecting crime, the work of the courts in providing justice for both victim and accused, and the work of the penal system in creating forms of punishment for the guilty. The timechart lays out the key moments of change and demonstrates how the government took on more responsibilty for dealing with crime in this period.

Source D Timechart: reforms in law enforcement, 1823–1907

1823	Gaols Act	Laid down standards for public gaols
1829	Metropolitan Police Act	Set up the first government-run police force in London
1830–34	Henry Brougham as Lord Chancellor	Reformed court procedures and introduced salaries for officers
1835	Municipal Corporation Act	Allowed town corporations to set up police forces like the one in London
1839	County Constabulary Act	Allowed police forces to be established in counties
1839	Prisons Act	Laid down further rules for prison discipline and education
1846	County Courts Act	Set up county courts for minor civil actions – quick and cheap
1848	Setting up of Court of Crown Cases Reserved	Allowed judges to consult on points of law before sentencing
1856	County and Borough Police Act	Establishment of police forces made compulsory
1865	Prisons Act	Extended government control and discipline rules to local prisons
1873	Judicature Act	Reorganised central court system including House of Lords as final court of appeal in civil cases
1877	Prisons Act	Extended national systems, including education and rehabilitation to all prisons
1879	Director of Public Prosecutions appointed	Government and police taking responsibility for prosecuting criminals – for the first time since the Roman Empire
1907	Court of Criminal Appeal set up	Allowed appeal by criminals on the basis of new evidence or conduct of trials

Questions

1 Rearrange the Acts listed in Source **D** in three columns, headed Police, Courts and Punishment.

2 What changes do these arrangements suggest in attitudes to law enforcement and the punishment of criminals?

3 Why did so many changes occur in this period?

4 Why did the process take so many Acts over so many years?

The early police force

▶ *How did policing develop?*

The Metropolitan Police

Set up in 1829 and based in a house backing onto Scotland Yard, the Metropolitan Police was under the control of two commissioners, Colonel Sir Charles Rowan and a lawyer, Sir Richard Mayne. It was to have 3,000 men, spread through seventeen divisions, each with 144 constables controlled by a superintendant. All had to be under thirty-five, at least 5 feet 5 inches (1.65 m) tall, healthy and able to read and write. Pay was low (see Source **A**) and the work involved walking a ' beat' (set area) of about twenty miles (32 km) a day, seven days a week. The uniform (see Source **B**) was designed to look civilian rather than military, and the constables had no other special protection.

Source A Table showing PC Andrews' weekly budget, 1853

	£ s d
Wages	1 1 0
Rent	4 6
Bread	5 0
Flour	1 0
Tea	1 0
Sugar	8
Other food, excluding meat	3 1 1
Wood, candles, coal	1 8
School fees	4

That left him with 2s 11d to pay for clothing, medicine etc. for himself, his wife and five children.

Source B Peelers in uniform. On the right is a Metropolitan Police inspector; on the left a policeman. They wore dark blue uniforms, with white or light grey trousers in summer. The cane frames of their hats gave them protection from attack; the men also carried truncheons and rattles (whistles were issued in 1884).

They faced hostility from a suspicious populace who often resented the new controls. Source **C** shows the kind of propaganda that they faced. JPs often resented them because they did not control the force, and obstructed them in court. Most recruits were working class, and of the first 2,800 recruited, 2,200 later resigned or were dismissed.

Source C Anti-police poster, 1830

Peel's Police,
RAW LOBSTERS
Blue Devils,
Or by whatever other appropriate
Name they may be known.

Notice is hereby given,

That a Subscription has been entered into, to supply the **PEOPLE** with **STAVES** [clubs] of a superior Effect, either for Defence or Punishment, which will be in readiness to be gratuitously [free of charge] distributed whenever a similar unprovoked, and therefore unmanly and bloodthirsty Attack, be again made upon Englishmen, by a Force unknown to the British Constitution, and called into existence by a Parliament illegally constituted, legislating for their individual interests, consequently in opposition to the Public good.

But the new force did make progress. Their value was recognised, especially when they took on a new responsibility for bringing prosecutions on behalf of victims. However, their role included crowd control, and in 1833 about 500 constables were called out to deal with a political demonstration in Cold Bath Fields. They were stoned by the mob and three were stabbed. One, PC Robert Culley, died of his wounds, and at the subsequent trial the jury brought in a verdict of 'justifiable homicide'; the government blamed the Metropolitan Police commissioners. Most people considered this unfair and public opinion reacted in favour of the police. By 1851 *Punch* magazine commented that the police 'were beginning to take their place in the affections of the people'. This all helped to bring police work to the attention of a wider public, and some councils hired them out to establish a force in their own area. When borough and county police forces were established, the Metropolitan Police were used as a model.

Detective work

At first there was a lot of resistance to detective work involving plain clothes constables, who seemed like government spies. When Sgt Popay disguised himself as a worker in 1833 to investigate the National Political Union of the Working Classes, at whose demonstration PC Culley was stabbed, the public outcry almost matched that for Culley. Attitudes began to change, however, and eight plain clothes detectives were appointed in 1842. The process was greatly speeded up by the development of the Fenian Society in Ireland; the Fenians, forerunners of the IRA, were willing to use force to win freedom from British rule (see Source **D**). In 1867 they rescued two members who were being transported to Clerkenwell prison, shooting one policeman dead, an attack that could have been prevented by police detectives and intelligence work. Thereafter the public was more responsive, and in 1877 a Criminal Investigation Department (CID) was set up with 200 men. By 1883 this was increased to 800: a new branch of policing – and fiction writing! – was born.

Source D A cartoon from *Punch* showing what many British people thought of the Fenians[

Questions

1 Why was a professional police force established first in London?

2 Consider Source **C** in the context of attitudes to law enforcement. Why was there so much hostility towards the police?

3 Why did the police gradually become accepted?

Local police forces

► *Why did police reform spread so slowly?*

The police forces in Lancashire and Yorkshire

In 1836 a parliamentary commission began to investigate policing in rural areas. Its report, much influenced by Edwin Chadwick, who was a follower of Jeremy Bentham, recommended the establishment of county police forces. Although this encouraged reformers to establish their own police forces, the best argument for doing so was simply the growth of crime and the inadequacy of the existing arrangements (see Source **A**). There were, however, many barriers to improvement, as Sources **B** and **C** suggest.

Source A Little enthusiasm for reform in Lancashire

▼

Many county JPs lacked interest and awareness of the extent of rural problems, and only Wigan, Liverpool and Preston had shown enthusiasm for reform. Liverpool had a day police consisting of one superintendent, 44 constables and 17 assistants. The night watch had a superintendent, 16 captains, 130 watchmen (of whom 45 were unfit and 25 hardly qualified) and 19 assistants. Preston had three policemen and a night watch, while Ashton-under-Lyne relied on the traditional arrangements made by the Court Leet.

Adapted from E.C. Midwinter, *Law and Order in Early Victorian Lancashire*, 1968

Source B Objections to the police

▼

Objections came from all the expected quarters. Many Tories and some Whigs [Liberals] were fearful of state control; northern manufacturers hated any meddling with freedom to trade; the popular press stirred up a fiery opposition; and many JPs and local councils resented the loss of their powers. The lower classes saw the 'blue-butchers' as yet another tool of oppression.

Adapted from E.C. Midwinter, *Law and Order in Early Victorian Lancashire*, 1968

Source C Rivalries in Manchester and Bolton

▼

Lancashire towns had to be incorporated as boroughs so that they could organise their own forces, or be swallowed up in the county force. In Manchester and Bolton, police reform was caught up in a political struggle between factions for and against incorporation. Manchester was incorporated in 1838, and the new council raised a force of 343 men. However, the Police Commissioners refused to dissolve their existing night police and the Court Leet its day police, so by 1839 Manchester had three rival police forces, and difficulty in raising the necessary £20,000 police rate. There were similar rivalries in Bolton. In the end, a special Act of parliament was required to sort out the mess, and the boroughs of Manchester and Bolton were finally able to run their own police from 1842.

Adapted from E.C. Midwinter, *Law and Order in Early Victorian Lancashire*, 1968

The policing of York, for example, was initially handled by three separate authorities. In July 1836 the Watch committee wanted to engage a London policeman to reorganise and superintend the York police, but was strongly opposed. The view was that York already possessed an able chief of police in the person of William Pardoe. In September 1836 Inspector Stuart arrived from London and recommended that the city be policed by a force of 24 men, later reduced to 21, at an estimated cost of £1,200 a year. The council opposed this on the grounds of expense, and voted for the force that already existed, superintended by William Pardoe.

Despite the problems of prejudice, political squabbles and reluctance to spend the rate-payers' money, police reform did make gradual progress, as Source **D** indicates. However, Source **E** reveals the limits of police effectiveness, and shows the continuing need for private initiatives. By 1856, when the government finally passed legislation making police forces compulsory, Lancashire had some 2,447 police; of these, 2,167 (88%) were in three forces – the county police, Manchester and Liverpool forces. Outside London its police represented one third of the national total. By 1857 only twenty-two authorities had developed county-wide forces.

Name of force	Date of inauguration	Population of city	Strength of force when first established	Strength in 1856
Lancashire County Constabulary	1839	995,301	502	614
Lancaster	1824	10,144	9	10
Wigan	1836	20,774	6	23
Liverpool	1836	205,954	290	886
Preston	1836	36,336	7	40
Manchester	1842	242,983	398	554
Bolton	1842	49,763	22	26
Salford	1844	53,200	31	95
Warrington	1847	22,894	5	9
Ashton	1848	30,676	13	23
Oldham	1849	52,820	12	22
Blackburn	1852	46,536	12	29

Source D Table showing the development of Lancashire police forces

Source E A poster of 1843 put out by the City of York Association for Prosecuting Felons, Cheats, etc.

CITY OF YORK ASSOCIATION
FOR PROSECUTING
FELONS, CHEATS, &c.
£5 Reward
Will be paid by the above Association, on Conviction of the Perpetrator of the undermentioned Felony, viz.
Slaughtering last Night, a
SHEEP
Belonging to MR. ROBINSON, Farmer, Osbaldwick, and Stealing the Carcass, leaving only the Skin and Entrails.
This Reward will be paid or distributed to or amongst such Person or Persons as shall give Information leading to the Offender's Conviction.
By Order,
J. BAYLDON,
Solicitor to the Association.
York, 4th December, 1843.

The policemen

Much also depended on the quality of policemen. The Lancashire County Constabulary was fortunate in having John Woodford as the Chief Constable, an earnest and efficient soldier who established good discipline and took care for the welfare of his men. When it came to the lower ranks, however, the situation was different. It was an unpopular, dangerous and arduous job. The level of pay only attracted recruits from the working classes, who were exactly the people with greatest reason to be suspicious of the new forces.

Superintents' salaries rarely fell below £100 per year, and rose as high as £300, whereas sergeants never earned more than £70. The normal weekly wage for a constable was 16–18 shillings (80–90p), although by 1856 many were earning a pound or more. By comparison, in 1860 skilled men in the iron trades earned over 30 shillings (£1.50) a week, miners around 25 shillings and bricklayers from 18 to 21 shillings. A family of five required about 30 shillings to live adequately.

Of the first two hundred recruits, fifty were discharged within six months, thirty of them for drunkenness. Many had to retire injured, usually with pensions of 1s or 1s 1d (6p) a day. The Rochdale Improvement Commissioners sent a report to the Home Secretary about three county policemen who had abused and threatened Alice Roberts in the Three Crowns Inn, Rochdale, one of them going so far as to thrust his head up her petticoats. The Commission were very worried and complained bitterly at 'this glaring act of oppression and tyranny'.

The aim of the 1839 County Constabulary Act had been to produce a national police force of trained and disciplined experts, to control the population and defeat crime. What developed was a local patchwork of forces, variable in quality, which demonstrated the need for central control and standardisation. In 1856 parliament made the provision of adequate police by local authorities compulsory, and the first inspection of local forces took place. This revealed that 120 forces were inadequate, but it also started the process of systematic improvement.

Questions

1 Why were many people suspicious of the new police?

2 What other factors made it difficult to establish effective police forces in Britain?

3 Explain how the different problems would work together to hinder development.

4 Why, therefore, did police reform gradually spread?

Police and public order

▶ *How well did the police keep order?*

The Chartists and the Rebecca Riots

The new police had an important role in maintaining public order. The Peterloo Massacre demonstrated what problems could occur in this age of popular protest. As long as the working classes could not vote, political demonstrations would persist. From 1839 fears of rural unrest caused by Chartism (Source **A**) and the Rebecca Riots (Source **B**) gave further impetus to the setting up of county police forces.

Source A   The Chartists

The Chartists' desire to democratise the parliamentary system was expressed in peaceful marches, petitions and demonstrations. Some became impatient with this and tried to organise armed revolution – for the middle and upper classes, however, the peaceful demonstrations were already frightening enough.

From R. Ellis, *People, Power and Politics*, vol. 2, 1995

Source B   A contemporary artist's impression of the Rebecca Riots

Source C   A meeting of the Reform League at Hyde Park, London, 1866

This meeting was to claim that 'intelligent and honest men' had a right to assemble anywhere. Over 1,600 policemen guarded the locked park gates. Some demonstrators turned back, but others tore down the railings. Many policemen were seriously hurt and the troops had to be called out. In 1872 Parliament recognised the right of demonstrators to meet in Hyde Park. Soap-box orators use it to this day.

From R. Whiting, *Crime and Punishment*, 1986

The Chartist movement aimed at parliamentary reform. Their basic demand was that working men should be able to vote and become MPs. Although most Chartists tried to achieve these aims through peaceful demonstration and petitioning parliament, there were some violent clashes. A rising in Newport in 1839 resulted in troops firing into the crowd, killing twenty-two people.

The Rebecca Riots in South Wales in 1839 were caused by rising charges for the new turnpike roads. The rioters set out to destroy turnpike gates, and dressed as women to disguise themselves. After 1843 turnpike charges were reduced. These rioters represented direct action against a specific grievance, unlike the wider political aims of the Chartists.

The baton charge

Public order became more complex as public meetings and marches increased. These meetings only involved a crime if they were held in defiance of magistrates' orders, or unless the crowd refused to disperse after the Riot Act was read. Authority still treated them all as hostile. The police formed the first line in containing the protesters – a difficult task for them, and one that contributed to their early unpopularity (see Source **C**).

But if public meetings were to continue, new methods of control were needed, and this was recognised by reformers as well as police. The radical, Francis Place, provided the police with their most effective method – the baton charge. With the help of responsible leaders and better organisation, protests became more peaceful and the police were able to handle such occasions, as Source **D** shows.

Source D A peaceful march in Manchester, organised by the craft unions in demand of a union for agricultural workers, 1874

The twentieth century

Demonstrations in the early twentieth century were either peaceful or not depending on how they were handled by those involved. When striking miners rioted at Tonypandy in 1910, the Home Secretary, Winston Churchill, refused to send troops in, and the police contained it. A year later, in Liverpool, a peaceful march broke up in disarray when the police were attacked by hooligans. The crowd then dispersed, leaving two dead.

In general there was a harsh response to demonstrations, and in the years of Depression after the First World War the government seemed willing to continue this approach. Although Churchill recommended using troops, the 1926 General Strike was remarkably peaceful. Source **E** shows the ultimate act of peaceful protest – the Jarrow March of 1936. The job of policing mass demonstrations remains a difficult one. Much depends on tact and self-discipline among both police and protestors.

Nevertheless, mistakes still occurred. Throughout October 1887, groups of unemployed people had been organised by the Social Democratic Federation to gather around the Red Flag in Trafalgar Square. Although the meetings were peaceful the authorities were becoming irritated by the time and expense of policing them, and in November the Home Secretary closed the square. A huge march resulted in campaigners trying to occupy the square. Police attempts to prevent this led to a riot, called Bloody Sunday, in which two protestors died and forty-seven police were injured.

Source E Unemployed workers from Jarrow, near Newcastle, march to London in 1936 to draw attention to their problems. The march was orderly and peaceful and drew great sympathy wherever it passed, but no action from government or parliament was forthcoming.

Questions

1 How did the aims and methods of the Chartists and the Rebecca rioters differ?

2 Which was more difficult for the police to deal with?

3 In what circumstances did protest become crime?

4 There is only one policeman shown in the picture of the Jarrow March (Source **E**). Does this mean that protest was more peaceful with a smaller police presence?

5 'Things would have been worse without them.' Is this a fair assessment of the police role in maintaining public order in this period?

Crime and criminals

 Did crime change in the nineteenth century?

The 'criminal class'

The nature of crime reflected the changes in society caused by industrial and technological development. Crime was still widespread, as Sources **A** and **B** show, but more significant was the nature of the criminal involved. Society concluded there was a new criminal class.

The emergence of a criminal class was encouraged by the growth of large towns, with mobile populations in lodging houses and in the poorest areas. This provided both gang members and their victims. Although often drawn from the working class, the criminal class was quite distinct from it. Many members were abandoned or orphaned children, and few lived to old age. Sources **C** to **F** illustrate the Victorian belief in the criminal class.

Source A Crime in Lancashire, based on the Constabulary Report, 1839

Dowling of the Liverpool police gave evidence of canal robberies. Robert Orrell testified to the fear of violence felt by Lancashire manufacturers; Thomas Bart, a straw-hat salesman, said that travellers felt least secure in 'the neighbourhoods of the northern manufacturing towns'. The roads across Blackstone Edge and Todmorden Vale were never used, for the people thereabouts were 'barbarous to an unusual degree' ... while the Wirral district and coast was a centre for wreckers.

Source B Railway crime in 1885: the evidence of a female detective against John Burgoyne, who was charged with the theft of a clergyman's bag

By direction of the stationmaster I placed myself in the waiting-room and saw the prisoner come into the room. I saw him lift up a case from under the table, put it down again, and go out onto the platform, but return almost immediately, and, taking up the case, go quickly out with it. He was dressed very shabbily, and had on shoes that prevented him being heard while walking. This excited my suspicions and ... I followed him.

Source C A London rookery in the nineteenth century

Source D Remarks by Henry Mayhew in *London Labour and the London Poor*, which was published in 1851–6

At the top of the Criminal Class were the 'Swell Mob' ... who would travel on cross-channel ships in the spring before returning for the racing and fair seasons in Britain. They travelled in first class railway carriages to con the occupants. Thimble-riggers and card-sharps often wore clerical collars.

Source E Cartoon from *Punch* magazine, 1851, suggesting the ways in which the criminal class recruited

THE DEALER IN OLD CLOTHES
TEACHING THE YOUNG IDEA HOW TO STEAL.

Source F Rev. H.W. Holland writing on 'professional thieves' in the *Cornhill Magazine*, 1862

Nearly all habitual thieves, male and female, die of consumption, and under or about thirty-five years of age. Drink, debauchery, irregular hours, the sudden transitions from luxury to a low prison diet – these things soon kill them off.

Such fears were greatly exaggerated. 'Respectable' society viewed slum areas, with their narrow streets and courtyards, known as 'rookeries', from a safe distance, and with fascinated horror, but the police found that these living conditions concentrated criminals in particular areas and made them easier to observe. Some historians believe there were too few gangs to constitute a 'criminal class'. Social reform and rising standards of living gradually eased the problems of the poor in general, while better policing was seen as the way to deal with the 'hardened' criminal.

New crimes – new aids to policing

Street robberies were common in large towns until the 1820s, when new gas street-lighting made it more difficult. Highway robbery declined everywhere as the introduction of turnpikes and an increase in traffic made the risks greater. New technology, such as the development of the railways, created new opportunities for crime (as seen in Source **B**), but also helped in the fight against it. Examples of the dual effect of new technology are shown in Source **G**.

Source G Technology: a double-edged weapon in the fight against crime

It was evident from the beginning that the Industrial Revolution represented a double-edged weapon in the fight against crime. Coining [forgery], an obsessive fear of earlier centuries, at first became more difficult as the Royal Mint developed new techniques, then easier as electroplating introduced new possibilities of home production. An unending struggle began between safe-manufacturers and safe-breakers, with every improvement provoking a new method of getting round it.

From J. Briggs et al., *Crime and Punishment in England*, 1996

Professional police forces made a difference as they provided a body of enforcers who had a professional interest in developing new methods of policing. From the 1850s onwards criminals began to be photographed, which helped in future identification. The development of telegraph and telephone links allowed information to travel faster than criminals. In 1901 the police began to fingerprint suspects, providing a unique personal identification. The twentieth century has seen many more technological aids to policing, including DNA 'fingerprinting'.

Questions

1 What types of crime and criminals are described in these sources?

2 What evidence suggests that new crimes developed in this period?

3 How far did new technology **a)** help and **b)** hinder law enforcement?

4 Refer back to earlier sections on crime in London. How far do you think crime there changed in the nineteenth century?

Changes in punishment

▶ *How and why did punishment change in this period?*

The prisons

The tendency for the death sentences laid down by the Bloody Code to be commuted (changed) to imprisonment or transportation (see p. 90) meant that prisons were increasingly used for punishment rather than to hold criminals awaiting trial. Pressure on prison space was rising from the 1770s on, and from 1776 disused warships moored at naval dockyards were used. Known as 'hulks', they provided appalling conditions (see Source **A**).

There was also a growing belief that criminals could be reformed, and Benthamite thinking encouraged this (see p. 78). Sources **B** and **C** illustrate the attitude of reformers, and Sources **D** and **E** and the two information panels provide examples of their work. Prison reform did not succeed overnight, but it did achieve a number of changes, such as the 1823 Gaols Act which laid down rules and standards for aspects of prisons. When a government report revealed continuing problems in 1835, further Acts were passed. In 1866 the Howard Association, named after the prison reformer John Howard, was established to monitor treatment of prisoners. In 1921 it merged with another such group, the Prison Reform League, to form the Howard League for Penal Reform, which is still active today.

Source B From Thomas Robe, *Some Considerations for Rendering the Punishment of Criminals More Effectual*, 1733

> Thus Justice, managed as an act of mercy, by slow and yet effectual methods, will bring Criminals to a sense of their crimes, and beget in them such a habit of industry, as in the end will make them useful, if not honest members of the public.

Source C A remark of Sir George Paul, prison reformer

> Few men have been hanged for a felony who might not have been saved to the community by the correction of a former misdemeanour.

Source A A prison hulk at Deptford, early nineteenth century

Source D Adapted from John Howard's report on Gloucester Gaol, 1777

Only one court[yard] for all prisoners; and one small day room, 12 ft by 11, for men and women felons. The free ward for debtors is 19 ft by 11, which having no window, has part of the plaster wall broke down for air. The night-room for men felons, up many steps, is close and dark; and the floor is so ruinous that it cannot be washed. The whole prison is out of repair. Many prisoners died here in 1773, and eight died about Christmas of the smallpox. No infirmary. There is no proper separation of the women. The licentious intercourse of the sexes is shocking to decency and humanity. Five or six children lately born in the gaol.

Sir George Paul (1746–1820)

Sir George Paul became High Sheriff of Gloucestershire in 1780, three years after Howard's damning report on the county gaol, housed in Gloucester Castle. He employed William Blackburn to design and build a new county prison and four houses of correction. He ensured that the place was secure, that prisoners were separated according to age and sex, and that proper health arrangements prevailed. The purpose of these arrangements was the reform and rehabilitation of the criminals. Work was hard and discipline strict, but some education and instruction was available. Paul's system achieved considerable success in reforming prisoners, and was copied in a number of American prisons.

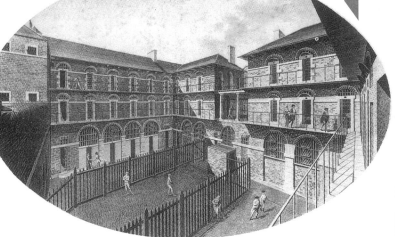

Source E The new county gaol, Gloucester

Elizabeth Fry (1780–1845)

Elizabeth Fry was a Quaker and became gaol visitor to Newgate prison in London. She found the conditions as appalling as any. Three hundred women were crammed into two rooms and two night-cells, with no privacy. It was, she said, 'more like a slave ship …The begging, swearing, gaming, fighting, singing, dancing, were too bad to be described.' Elizabeth arranged for the women to be given Bible instruction and taught to sew. She later formed a Ladies Prison Committee to help in the work at Newgate and began to inspect other prisons.

Questions

1 What arguments did reformers put forward to explain the need for reform?

2 What evidence suggests that they were concerned and motivated by:
a) mercy and justice; b) religion and morality;
c) efficiency?

3 What changes in British society in the eighteenth and early nineteenth centuries encouraged these ideas?

4 Using this information, explain which of the reformers' arguments would have been most convincing to nineteenth-century governments and public opinion.

Transportation

Penal reform brought some improvements for convicted criminals, but changes were limited and often slow. Transportation to America had ceased after the War of Independence in 1776, but was gradually replaced by transportation to Australia. The first convicts went to Botany Bay in 1788. Transportation to Australia involved even longer voyages and dreadful conditions (see Source **F**).

Source F On board a convict ship

Source G Letter from a convict in Australia to his father, 1835

We have as much to eat as we like, as some masters are a great deal better than others. All a man has got to mind is to keep a still tongue in his head, and do his master's duty; but if he don't he may as well be hung at once, for they would take you to the magistrates' court and get a hundred lashes, and then get sent to a place called Port Arthur to work in irons for two or three years ... then, thank God for it, I am doing a great deal better than I was at home.

Your Committee considers ... that Transportation is not a simple punishment, but rather a series of punishments, embracing every degree of human suffering, from the lowest, consisting of a slight restraint upon freedom of action, to the highest, consisting of long and tedious torture; and that the average amount of pain inflicted upon offenders in consequence of a sentence of Transportation is very considerable.

Source H From the report of the 1837 Select Committee of the House of Commons

In Australia, conditions for the prisoners were variable. Some convicts were hired out to settlers, while others remained in barracks on the convict settlements. Conditions were generally worse in the barracks. After four years in them they could earn a ticket of leave, and later, depending on the length of their original sentence, could achieve conditional and absolute pardons. Only with an absolute pardon could they return to Britain. Sources **G** and **H** indicate the treatment that convicts received. For the strong and lucky, transportation could be an opportunity for a new life, but for many it meant years of suffering followed by death in a foreign land.

A parliamentary committee of 1837 disapproved of the suffering of convicts, the costs and the uncertain results of the system. Australians also resented being used as a dumping-ground, and from 1840 transportation was abandoned.

Questions

1 Why was transportation abandoned as a form of punishment?

2 Using your knowledge of Victorian attitudes to interpret Sources **F** to **H**, did this happen because of humanitarian concerns (mercy and justice) or political pressures?

Prison reform

▶ *Why was it difficult to reform prison conditions?*

Problems in the prisons

Growing use of prison as a punishment and the end of transportation increased concern with prison conditions and the need to promote reform and the rehabilitation of the criminal. Several methods were tried, of which the best known were the Separate System and the Silent System. Neither was successful.

Reform was limited because people continued to believe that criminals deserved the harshest punishments, and that punishment should be for deterrence and retribution. In addition, reform was expensive and it was difficult to convince government to spend scarce resources on it. Sometimes well-meaning mistakes were made, and effective rehabilitation for a varied convict population was difficult. As all the sources in this unit demonstrate, the result was that prisons remained grim and desolate places, and a destructive form of punishment.

Source A Prison work

▼

Useful work was considered either impossible or undesirable, and prisoners were kept occupied in such pointless tasks as turning the treadwheel and crank. The treadwheel was a big iron frame of steps around a revolving cylinder; the crank was a wheel, like that of a paddle steamer fitted into a box of gravel, which the prisoner had to turn by means of a handle. They were a means of occupation which would not threaten the livelihood of honest men and which were purposeless.

Adapted from C. Hibbert, *The English*, 1994

Source B A treadmill at Wormwood Scrubs prison, around 1890

The Separate System and the Silent System

The Separate System was based on the work of Sir George Paul at Gloucester, but some unfortunate changes were made in the light of American experiments. Paul had isolated prisoners when they first came to Gloucester, then gradually allowed them to mix as rehabilitation progressed. The Separate System, however, isolated them completely, and for the whole of their sentence – effectively they suffered years of solitary confinement.

Pentonville was built in 1842 as a model prison of this kind. It provided each prisoner with his own cell, in which he lived and worked. Only for short periods of exercise, and Sunday chapel, did prisoners come together, and then elaborate measures were used to prevent any contact (see Source **C**). The chapel had individual cubicles so that prisoners could not see one another. Not surprisingly, many prisoners could not cope with the isolation; in the first eight years after Pentonville opened, 22 prisoners went insane, 26 had nervous breakdowns and 3 committed suicide.

Source C The Separate System in operation: the exercise yard at Pentonville

Source D The Silent System in operation at Coldbath Fields prison, Middlesex

Millbank prison built in 1821, utilised the Silent System, in which prisoners were housed in separate cells and forbidden to speak to one another during the first half of their sentence (see Source **D**). The Silent System was widely adopted after the expensive failure of the Separate System of individual cells at Pentonville.

Because criminals re-offended many people believed that rehabilitation was impossible; this was reinforced by Victorian beliefs that science could identify a 'criminal type'. One surgeon said that criminals had lighter brains, and that 'enormous jaws, high cheek bones, prominent eyebrows, arches, solitary lines on the palms, extremely large eye-sockets and handle shaped or flattened ears' were common in criminals, savages and apes.

The Prison Acts of 1865 and 1877 brought all prisons under the control of the Home Office, under a system of 'hard labour, hard fare and a hard board'. What this meant is indicated in Sources **E** and **F**. In fact this harsh system proved ineffective, and in 1898 a new inquiry was held which recommended more humane treatment. Provisions such as an end to flogging and better prison clothes were gradually adopted in the twentieth century.

Source E The 1865 Prison Act

According to the 1865 Act, prisoners could be: 1. Confined in a cell for nine months; 2. Given hard labour, including: treadwheel, crank/capstan; shot drill (moving piles of cannon shot), stonebreaking, oakum picking; 3. Kept in close confinement on bread and water for three days (a month plus whipping if ordered by a Justice); 4. Kept in irons; 5. Given a board bed rather than a hammock.

Adapted from R. Whiting, *Crime and Punishment*, 1986

Source F From the Royal Commission on Prisons, 1879

At Chatham prisoners severely mutilated themselves and threw themselves beneath the wheels of the railway wagons in the dock basins in their efforts to escape from the fearful place. If they did not die, they were flogged. 'There was no reason', said the Governor, 'why they should not be flogged, because they had only mutilated an arm or a leg.'

The treatment of juveniles

Evidence shows us that many offenders were below the age of twenty-one, and often little more than children. The social changes of the Industrial Revolution undermined family links, and orphaned or abandoned children had little choice but to turn to crime. London was notorious for its street children (see Source **G**); Dr Barnardo, who founded the charity to help them, estimated that there were 30,000 children sleeping rough in London in 1876. The problem was not confined to London, however, or even to the larger cities.

The cruelty of treating children in the same way as adult criminals was recognised, however, and Source **H** describes some early efforts at change. Nevertheless, as Sources **I** and **J** illustrate, progress was patchy and variable.

Source H   The treatment of young offenders

As early as 1818, magistrates in Birmingham were sentencing some juveniles. Parkhurst Prison opened on the Isle of Wight in 1838 and there was a separate wing for young offenders. In 1854 the Youthful Offenders Act provided some government assistance for special reform schools, and allowed young offenders to be sent there for two to five years after a short prison sentence. In 1857 young vagrants could be sent direct to 'industrial schools' to learn the skills required for employment.

Adapted from C. Emsley, *Crime and Society in England, 1750–1900*, 1987

Source I   From the records of the Howard League

1876 – a poor, motherless boy of only 7 years of age was charged with rolling in a barley field. The weeping boy was fined and sent to prison.

Source J   Sentencing policies

There was no common sentencing policy across the country, and the number of places in reform schools varied from one locality to another. Locality and gender both appear to have influenced sentencing: more urban than rural offenders were sent to prison, more boys than girls, and a disproportionately large number of Irish children.

From C. Emsley, *Crime and Society in England, 1750–1900*, 1987

Source G   London street children in about 1900

Progress only really began in the twentieth century. In 1902 an experimental training school for young offenders was established in the village of Borstal, in Kent. It proved very successful. In 1908 a Children's Act banned prison sentences for those under the age of fourteen, and the Prevention of Crime Act ordered training schools modelled on the Borstal experiment to be established for fifteen to twenty-one-year-olds. In 1932 these were reorganised into a single system of Approved Schools.

But rehabilitation of juvenile criminals faced the same problems as for adults: lack of money, overcrowding and the establishment of a criminal pecking order undermined the work. As the governor of one Borstal said in 1978, 'You cannot take somebody and give him forty-two weeks in Borstal to put right eighteen or nineteen years of neglect, disturbance and deprivation.' Borstals and Approved Schools were later replaced by arrangements for youth custody.

Questions

1. What factors made prison reform difficult to achieve?

2. Explain how different factors worked together to prevent reform.

3. How did treatment of juvenile criminals change between 1800 and 1950?

4. What problems limited the effectiveness of reform in this area?

Women and crime

 ### How were female criminals regarded?

In pre-industrial Britain women were involved in a variety of crimes, such as murder, robbery, theft and prostitution. Apart from prostitution it is difficult to say that crime could be related to gender. There is evidence, however, that in industrial Britain some gender-related patterns began to emerge.

The image of woman

The Victorians had a strong sense of what women ought to be. In pre-industrial Britain their role involved far more than housework; upper-class ladies managed large numbers of servants and workers to meet the needs of an extended household, and the wives of peasants and labourers shared the work in the fields. The industrial revolution led to much greater opportunity for women to work independently but also created a conflict between the needs of work and family. Prosperity increased the numbers who could aspire to be middle class – and one of the defining factors of the middle class was that female members did not need to work outside the home. Thus the traditional image of women evolved into a highly restrictive middle-class ideal – 'the angel in the house'. Sources **A** to **C** illustrate the characteristics Victorian women were expected to display.

Source B Sarah Ellis, a Victorian writer, describes the position of women in 1845

As a woman, the first thing of importance is to be content to be below men – below them in mental power, in the same proportion that you are in bodily strength.

Source C John Ruskin, art historian and thinker, writing in 1865 on man and woman

The man is, above all, the doer, the creator, the discoverer, the defender. His mind is for thinking and invention. The woman's power is for rule [within the home] – and her mind is for sweet ordering, arrangement and decision. She must be lastingly, incorruptibly good; unfailingly wise ... not to improve herself, but to sacrifice herself.

The crimes of women

These images affected the role of women in crime, but precisely how is difficult to assess. According to the historian Clive Emsley, the proportion of women among those brought to trial fell in the nineteenth century. In the late seventeenth century, 45 per cent of those brought to trial at the Old Bailey were women, but by the early twentieth century this had fallen to 12 per cent. The trend seems undeniable and the numbers of women criminals who re-offended seems to have risen, making fewer women responsible for a larger proportion of female crime.

Victorian commentators, however, felt that female crime was increasing. Source **D**, a remark by a Victorian criminologist, provides an example of this. More significant is how those involved in crime were portrayed. Some women were violent, as Source **E** shows, but commentators were mostly concerned with those who abused their feminine role.

Source D A remark made by the criminologist L.O. Pike, 1876

In proportion as they have rendered themselves independent of men for their subsistence, they have thrown off the protection against competition and temptation which dependence on men implies. It follows that, so far as crime is determined by external circumstances, every step made by woman towards her independence is a step towards that precipice at the bottom of which lies a prison.

Source E From the *Hull Advertiser*, 1836, describing the arrest of Jane Smith for drunkenness and assaulting two police officers

The prisoner was of Amazonian build [like the mythical warrior-women], and had conducted herself more like a fury than anything else. She was obliged to be handcuffed and have her legs strapped together to keep her from kicking anyone she came near, and it took five men to convey her in a cart to the station house.

Source F The case of Eliza Higgins

In 1857, for example, Eliza Higgins, a 21-year-old domestic servant lodged in a London workhouse, was tried for the wilful murder of her baby daughter; the Old Bailey jury hearing the case found her guilty of manslaughter, recommended mercy, and commented that 'the bastardy laws have a strong tendency to increase this class of crime'.

From C. Emsley, *Crime and Society in England, 1750–1900*, 1987

Source G Josephine Butler, who campaigned to defend prostitutes and ensure fair treatment for them in prisons. Her most significant campaign was her fight against the Contagious Diseases Acts of 1866 and 1869, which allowed suspected prostitutes to be forced to undergo an examination to see if they had a sexually transmitted disease. If so, they could be locked up. Male clients were not subject to the same procedure.

Poisoning was seen as a female crime, practised by domestic servants or wives whose husbands died mysteriously. There was most concern with crimes challenging the ideal of womanhood. Penalties for abortion were increased after 1803, and in 1861 the woman seeking abortion was made guilty of a crime, as well as the abortionist. Women's crimes revealed a double standard in society – male juries were horrified by the crime, but reluctant to impose the full penalty of death on the female criminal. Source **F** provides an example.

The most harshly condemned female crime was prostitution. Although not in itself a crime, the associated crimes were soliciting, living off immoral earnings or running a 'house of ill fame'. Prostitutes, however, were regarded as the source of evil; they corrupted young men, tricked them, robbed them and destroyed them. They were the associates of thieves, the source of disease – in short, the complete opposite of what women should be. Although some campaigners attempted to help prostitutes (see Source **G**), only one other group were regarded with such loathing – the Suffragettes (see Case File, pp. 96–9).

Questions

1 Look at Sources **A** to **C**. What image of women did Victorian writers build up?

2 How does this explain the attitude shown in Source **D**?

3 In what ways do the attitudes shown in Sources **D** and **F** conflict?

4 How would you explain the conflicting attitudes?

5 How far do these attitudes explain why prostitutes were so harshly treated?

The Suffragettes

▶ *How successful were the Suffragettes?*

Women's rights

In the early nineteenth century women had virtually no rights. By the 1870s they had gained property rights, many personal rights and even education, but they still had no political rights. Women therefore campaigned for the right to vote. Some progress was made, and in 1890 Mrs Millicent Fawcett founded the National Union of Women's Suffrage Societies (NUWSS), to campaign peacefully for the vote ('suffrage' is the right to vote). This group, known as the Suffragists, organised several major protest marches (see Source **A**).

By 1900 the majority of MPs claimed to support women's voting rights, but still parliament voted against it, and some women began to lose patience. In 1903 Emmeline Pankhurst and her daughters formed a breakaway group, the Womens' Social and Political Union (WSPU, nicknamed the 'Suffragettes'), which was prepared to use more drastic methods. They began by heckling and demonstrating at political meetings, as Source **B** describes, but then graduated to attacks on property, getting themselves arrested, refusing to pay fines and going on hunger strike when imprisoned. Sources **C** to **E** illustrate their tactics, which involved the deliberate use of crime to publicise their campaigns.

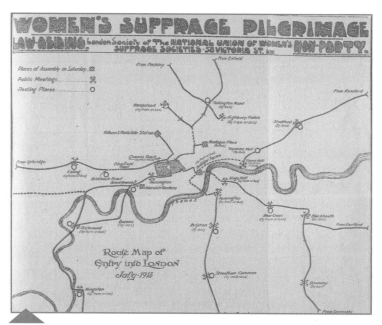

Source A A route map through London of the NUWSS march, 1913

Source B A description by Emmeline Pankhurst of how the Suffragettes disrupted a meeting held by the Prime Minister in 1905

▼

At the end of the meeting, Annie Kenney, who had been smuggled into the hall in disguise, called out ... 'Will the Liberal government give women the vote?' At the same moment, Theresa Billington let drop a huge banner with the words 'Will the Liberal government give justice to working women?' Just for a moment their was a gasping silence ... The Cabinet ministers did nothing. Then, amid uproar and shouting, the women were seized and flung out of the hall.

Source C Table showing the tactics of Suffragists and Suffragettes, 1905–10

Year	Suffragists	Suffragettes
1905	Held meetings in most constituencies prior to General Election	Heckling at meetings
1906		Deliberately got arrested and imprisoned, although committed no acts of violence
1907	Held first procession	Deliberately got arrested and imprisoned, although committed no acts of violence
1908	Led a deputation to see the Prime Minister	Started occasional attacks on property, such as breaking windows
1909	Arranged public debates	Suffragettes in prison went on hunger strike – several were force-fed
1910	Raised a petition of 280,000 signatures	Suffragettes in prison went on hunger strike – several were force-fed

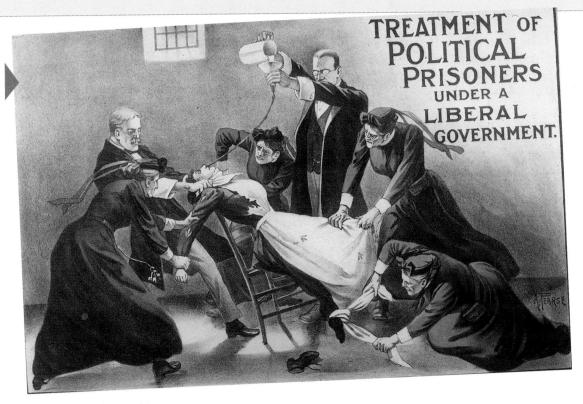

Source D
Force-feeding a Suffragette

TREATMENT OF POLITICAL PRISONERS UNDER A LIBERAL GOVERNMENT.

Source E A description by the Suffragette Lady Constance Lytton of being force-fed in prison. The experience left her with permanent damage to her heart.

Two of the wardresses took hold of my arms, one held my head and one my feet. I shut my mouth and clenched my teeth ... After trying with the wooden gag, the doctor finally had recourse to the steel one. He said if I resisted so much with my teeth he would have to feed me through the nose. The pain of it was intense, and at last I must have given way for he got the gag between my teeth, and turned it far more than necessary until my jaws were wide apart. Then he put the tube down my throat ... Then the food was poured in quickly ... It made me sick and I doubled up, but the wardresses instantly pressed back my head and the doctor leant on my knees. The horror of it was more than I can describe.

Source F The unpopularity of the Suffragettes

Votes for women remained unpopular. In 1909 a 'Men's League for Opposing Women's Suffrage' was formed. In 1908 a petition against votes for women gained 337,038 signatures. Only a small percentage of the 10.5 million women in the country joined suffrage movements, and some even campaigned against them. Many Suffragettes were violently and indecently assaulted; antagonistic men sexually harrassed them. A famous doctor remarked in 1912 that 'there is, mixed up with the women's movement, much mental disorder', while even Margaret Bondfield, an active trade unionist, said that she 'disliked votes for women as the hobby of disappointed old maids whom no one had wanted to marry'.

Adapted from Paula Bartley, *The Changing Role of Women*, 1996

So near to success

By 1911 the Suffragette tactics seemed to be paying off. The Liberal government introduced a bill into parliament to give women the vote, and it passed its first reading by a majority of 167. Then the government changed its mind as the Prime Minister, H.H. Asquith, was against it. Equally important in political terms, it was clear that many people were opposed to votes for women, as Source **F** illustrates. The bill was abandoned.

The Suffragettes were furious with the reverse in their political fortunes, and increased their campaign of crime (see Sources **G** and **H** on p. 98). Much of this, however, turned public opinion against the campaign, and fed the view of its opponents that women could not be trusted to vote. In 1913, when women's suffrage was again debated in parliament, it was defeated by forty-eight votes. And in 1913 the Suffragettes were deprived of one of their most effective weapons by the passing of the so-called Cat and Mouse Act to deal with hunger strikes.

Instead of being required to force-feed the women, the government were now allowed to order the temporary release of those who became ill; they could then be re-arrested and forced to serve the remainder of their sentence when they recovered. Source **I** shows the working of the Act in 1913.

Source G   Table showing Suffragette activity in May–June 1913

31 May	Railway telegraph wires cut in Cardiff and Monmouth
2 June	Postboxes in Lewisham set on fire
3 June	Boat-house in Oxford burnt down; acid poured onto the greens of a golf course near Doncaster
4 June	Emily Davison throws herself under the King's horse at the Derby
5 June	Purple dye poured into reservoirs near Bradford
9 June	Grandstand at Hurst Park racecourse in Surrey set on fire; cricket pavilion in Middlesex set on fire
18 June	Church in Rowley Regis set on fire
30 June	Railway station at Leuchars junction set on fire

From L. Bellamy and K. Moorse, *The Changing Role of Women*, 1996

Source H   A Suffragette is arrested in London

Source I   Table showing operation of the Cat and Mouse Act. At the time of the passing of the Act there were 13 people in prison.

Person in prison	Date sentenced (1913)	Offence	Sentence	Release	Remarks
1	9 Jan	Attack on letterbox	8 months	20 Aug	Sentence served
2	7 Feb	Breaking windows	5 months	9 June	Sentence served
3	21 Feb	Breaking windows	6 months	18 July	Sentence served
4	21 Feb	Breaking windows	4 months	30 April	Discharged when sentence half-served; no reason given
5	5 March	Setting fire to a pillarbox	9 months	28 April	Rearrested Aug 1913, Jan, June 1914
6	8 March	Setting fire to railway carriage	9 months	28 April	Force-fed 114 times
7	20 March	Breaking windows	5 months	29 July	Sentence served
8	27 March	Breaking windows	1 month	end April	Sentence served
9	4 April	Attempted arson	4 months	18 July	Sentence served
10	12 April	Found in possession of inflammatory materials	6 weeks	end April	Not rearrested
11			6 weeks	28 April	Rearrested Jan 1914
12	22 April	Damaging pictures at Manchester Art Gallery	5 months	21 May	Not rearrested
13			9 months	end June	Not rearrested

From R. Whiting, *Crime and Punishment*, 1986

The end of the campaign

By mid-1913 it was clear that the Suffragette campaign was a liability to the cause of women's suffrage. When Emily Wilding Davison attempted to disrupt the Epsom Derby, and died under the hooves of the King's horse, her sacrifice was condemned as irresponsible and dangerous. Source **J** shows the reaction of the press, and the comments made by Lloyd George (Source **K**), who was a supporter of women's rights, summed up the view of many.

By 1914 the Suffragettes were unable to give up the campaign but also unlikely to succeed through it. They were then given a new opportunity by the outbreak of war: they could give up their campaign as a patriotic gesture, and greatly strengthen the case for women's rights by their contribution to the war effort. In 1918 the right to vote was granted to middle-class women over thirty.

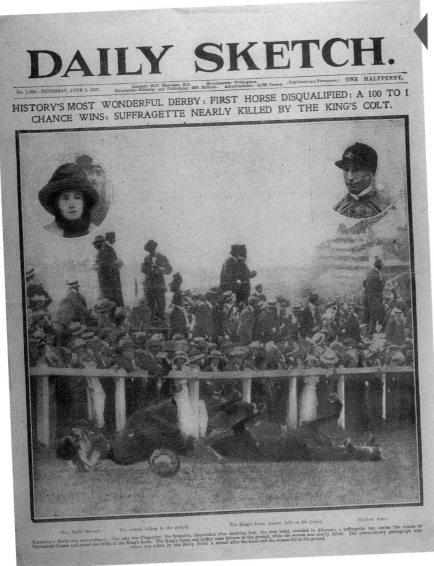

Source J The front page of the *Daily Sketch*, 5 June 1913, reporting the injury to Emily Davison, which was to prove fatal.

Source K David Lloyd George, Chancellor of the Exchequer, on the Suffragettes, 1913

Haven't the Suffragettes the sense to see that the very worst way of campaigning for the vote is to try to intimidate or blackmail a man into giving them what he would gladly give otherwise?

Questions

1 What crimes did the Suffragettes commit?

2 What did they hope to achieve by this campaign?

3 Which sources suggest that they succeeded?

4 Which sources indicate that they failed?

5 How would you reconcile this conflicting evidence to assess the overall effect of the Suffragettes?

6 Using Sources **B**, **E** and **F** together, describe the different attitudes adopted towards the Suffragettes by men.

7 How were they regarded by other women?

8 Using your knowledge of nineteenth-century attitudes and beliefs, explain why reactions to the Suffragettes were often so extreme.

9 The Suffragettes used criminal acts as a form of protest. How did they differ from earlier protest groups such as the Rebecca rioters, the Chartists and Trade Union marchers, who also broke the law?

10 How far do you consider that any of the protesters were justified in what they did?

15 Crime and punishment since 1950: a changing world

Overview

▶ **Have crime and punishment changed since 1950?**

In the period after the Second World War, the pace of social and political change has increased. To an extent this is the result of two world wars. Many changes had begun before 1914, but the need to develop new techniques of organisation, new technology and to harness natural resources influenced the speed of development. It was the total effect of two wars within a generation that created the world that we see today.

Attitudes and expectations

In the nineteenth century most people accepted the idea of social class and differences in wealth. While the working classes wanted new laws to improve living and working conditions, progress was slow. But the First World War changed this, as working-class men volunteered and fought and died in their thousands, often alongside officers from the upper class. And women did vital jobs on the home front as well, so that in 1918 few people could deny ordinary working men and women the right to vote. All men over twenty-one and some women over thirty were given the vote in 1918; this was extended to all women over twenty-one in 1928.

After 1918 new laws improved living and working conditions, but the government did little to ease the problems caused by the Depression of the 1930s. Improvements caused by the Second World War, such as full employment, were built on in peacetime. For example, free secondary education was made a right for all and the National Insurance Act provided unemployment and sickness benefit.

Employment and technology

After 1918 the techniques used to mass produce weapons were used for other products. In America, for example, Henry Ford set up the first assembly lines to produce cars more cheaply, enabling ordinary people to buy them (see Source **A**).

This was the beginning of the 'consumer revolution' – making goods for ordinary people to buy and encouraging demand for them through advertising. This spiral of growth began with the Second World War and continued until the 1970s.

A shrinking world

War revolutionised transport and communications, with the introduction of such things as television and computers on a wide scale. People became much more aware of foreign places, and after 1945 better prosperity and transport allowed people to travel abroad. In addition, new immigrants coming to Britain for work brought different cultures. Young people were particularly affected by these changes. Many left school at fifteen and, with good work available, had money to spend.

In 1956 a new kind of music – rock and roll – started to become popular, and teenagers developed 'their own style of dress, music and even language. They were targeted by advertisers and became new consumers. Their music and culture were international, and remain so today.

Until the 1960s this was a period of optimism, caused by better education, job opportunities and awareness of the wider world. Many people who had been oppressed gained civil rights, such as black people in the southern states of America. In Britain this mood was reflected in the Abortion Act of 1966, the legalisation of adult homosexuals and the abolition of capital punishment (except for treason) in 1965.

Source A The assembly line system producing Model T Ford cars

The crises of the 1970s

Attitudes changed in the 1970s; a world oil crisis raised the cost of energy and technology destroyed rather than caused jobs. Crime did not disappear, as a consumer society simply revealed the gap between rich and poor. There was concern about drug abuse, shoplifting and availability of alcohol, all often associated with young people and their music. New luxuries also created new crimes – theft of and from cars and drunk driving.

Politics changed, too, as people who felt they were denied basic rights took to extreme methods to acquire them. The Arab peoples, for example, were unable to defeat Israel in war and turned to terrorism and hijacking to draw attention to their problems. In Europe society had become more racially complex and many immigrants suffered racial discrimination, a situation made worse by unemployment.

Crime in Britain

In Britain these problems were expressed in various ways. Drug smuggling and hijacking demanded a sophisticated response from police and efforts at international co-operation. The failure of Ulster Catholics to gain civil rights led to terrorism in Northern Ireland from the IRA. Racial problems everywhere have led to an increase in racial attacks. In addition, alienation of political groups has caused crimes such as poll tax riots and protests against roads or weapons installations; many of these cause real problems for policing (see Source **B**).

The position of the police in our society has been affected by high-profile abuses of justice and corruption cases coming to light, and although the modern police are more effective than ever, public faith in them is not as high as it was. Many people are concerned about 'everyday' crimes such as vandalism, car theft, mugging or drug abuse. There is no doubt that crime figures have been rising since 1950, and a growing percentage of crimes are committed by young people. However, there are also fears not supported by statistics – that violence is increasing, that crime is race-related and that new crimes have been invented. Several causes have been cited:

- a breakdown in family values
- poor discipline in schools
- drugs and alcohol
- the failure to punish people properly.

The result is the existence of more fears and myths about crime and punishment, which makes for a confusing situation. For this reason the final section of this book does not attempt to summarise the history of crime and punishment since 1950, but to raise issues for debate. Some key questions are:

- Has crime changed with new or worse crimes, or are these old crimes in a new form?
- How valid is the evidence used to portray crime today, particularly in the media?
- Has punishment changed, particularly in failing to act as a deterrent?
- Has policing changed? Has the job become more difficult and why?

Use the evidence in the following pages to debate these issues in the light of your knowledge about crime and punishment through time.

▶ **Has crime changed since 1950?**

There are a number of popular preconceptions about crime in the last five decades, of which three in particular contribute to widespread concern. The first is that crime is increasing; the second is that it has become more violent; and the third is that new crimes have been invented.

The sources in this unit provide some examples of crime since 1950.

Source A   Shoplifting

▼

Shoplifting has doubled in each decade since 1960. In Plymouth in 1976, 417 persons were convicted: 218 males; 199 females. Of those convicted, 152 were under 29 years old; 98 were 50 or more years old; strangely 222 had more money on them than the stolen items cost.

From R. Whiting, *Crime and Punishment*, 1986

Source B   Fraud and similar crimes

▼

Fraud, tax evasion, computer manipulation, failure to maintain safety and health standards in factories, hotels and restaurants etc, can all be called 'white-collar crimes'. In fact there are many more convictions of working-class or unemployed people for fraudulent social security claims than there are of middle-class swindlers.

From R. Whiting, *Crime and Punishment*, 1986

Source C   With the Sex Discrimination Act in 1975, some job titles had to be changed, such as 'fireman' to 'firefighter'

▼

A career in the London Fire Brigade
A future worth considering.

You may not previously have considered the possibility – but the London Fire Brigade represents a career challenge not just for men but for women too.

In providing its services to the most ethnically diverse capital city in the world, the London Fire Brigade can offer women and men of all races and from a wide variety of backgrounds a uniquely rewarding mix of job satisfaction, good pay, opportunities for promotion and long term prospects. Women, like all recruits, join as firefighters, get the same chances to prove their ability and, if keen to do so, to make the most of their potential and go for promotion.

To become a London Firefighter you must live in Greater London, be 18–30 and physically fit, be at least 5′ 6″ tall, have a 36″ chest (with 2″ expansion) and good unaided eyesight.

If you would like to find out more about a career with the London Fire Brigade send for further information now by returning the coupon to:
London Fire Brigade,
Room 506,
Queensborough House,
Albert Embankment,
London SE1 7SD

Source D   Racist disturbances

▼

A series of disturbances were caused in London and Manchester during the summer and autumn by the activities of neo-Nazi and extreme right-wing organizations, leading to widespread demands for legislation banning incitement to racial hatred.

From *Keesing's Contemporary Archives*, December 1962

Source E   Headline from *The Times*, 8 July 1997

▼

Tehran ordered Lockerbie blast, says ex-Iran spy

Source F Should a doctor be allowed to turn off a life-support system if the patient wants to die? In some countries the doctor may face a murder charge for doing so.

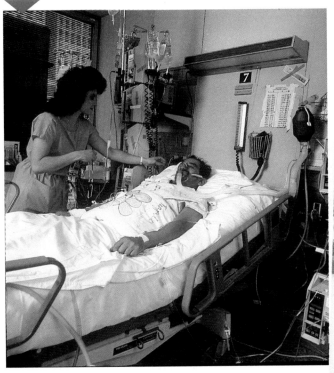

Source G Emil Savundra: after a long career of swindling, Emil Savundra was brought to trial in London in 1968. He was found guilty of fraud relating to motor insurance schemes and sent to prison for 10 years.

Source H From *The Times*, July 1997

Prison sentences for racially-motivated crimes of violence will be increased under new Government plans ... The harsher punishment is designed to show that the Home Office regards racist crime as 'hideous' and that it will not be tolerated ... Tougher new penalties are being drawn up for inclusion in the Crime and Disorder Bill, due to be published in the autumn, which will introduce a new offence of racial harrassment and racially-motivated violence.

Source I From *The Times*, 1997

RSPCA used gene test to track badger killers

Four men accused of killing a badger after digging it from its sett were linked to the crime by DNA tests on the animal's body, a court was told yesterday.

Source J Headline from *The Times*, 3 September 1997

Paparazzi are charged with manslaughter

Questions

1 Make a list of all the crimes described.

2 How many would you describe as new?

3 What other 'new' crimes can you think of?

4 How many could be described as old crimes carried out in a new setting?

5 What factors have encouraged 'new' crime?

6 How many of these crimes involve violence?

7 How far does the evidence in these sources support the concerns described earlier (top of p. 102)?

Evidence about crime

Can we believe what we read?

Evidence about crime comes in various forms. The main sources of information are statistics compiled by various bodies – the police, the Home Office and different pressure groups; anecdotal evidence – what people say about their own experiences; and articles written in the press or presented on television and radio. However, there are problems involved in relying on any of these sources, as a close examination of the examples in this unit will show.

Source A   Crimes and clear-up rates, 1971–82

Number of serious offences recorded by the police (000s)

	1971	1982
England and Wales	1665.7	3263.4
Scotland	211	435.1
Northern Ireland	30.8	62.1

Percentage of serious crimes 'cleared up' by the police

	1971	1982
England and Wales	45	37
Scotland	38	30
Northern Ireland	32	19

From J.M. Coutts et al., *Social Issues*, 1985

Source B   Crime and the media

The broadsheets report about three times the actual proportion of violent crime and the tabloids about ten times. The picture of the world that one gets from crime news is that it is a very violent place. Inflated perceptions of the level of violence create pressures for something to be done.

From R. Greaf, *Crime, Justice and the Media*, 1989

Source C   From the *Sun* newspaper, 1995

The Sun speaks its mind: murder of children is becoming almost commonplace in 1995. Our MPs should heed the voice of the people and bring back the death penalty for child murderers … Society demands vengeance, an eye for an eye.

Source D   Violent offences and the media

The increase in violent or sexual offences always receives headline treatment from the media and increases public anxiety. However these account for less than 5% of all crimes reported, and about 75% of all such crimes are cleared up by the police.

From J.M. Coutts et al., *Social Issues*, 1985

Source E   The recording of crime

In most cases all the figures show is that police are noting down more crimes in their notebooks than they used to, not that the number of crimes has increased. The irony is that the more efficient the police become the higher the recorded crime figures rise.

From J.M. Coutts et al., *Social Issues*, 1985

Source F   From the *Sunday Times*, 5 January 1997

(1)
INCREASINGLY there is concern that arrest and punishment through the courts are no longer automatic. 1955 … was the beginning of a sustained decline in the use of imprisonment that continued with only a few short interruptions for 38 years.
  During the period of the Great Decline, the number of reported crimes increased twelve-fold, while the number of people entering prison increased two and a half times. Add in the effects of shorter sentences, and the number of prisoners only doubled. Put such trends together, control for the size of the changing population, and the result is dramatic. This is not some minor change in policy of interest only to criminologists. The risk of going to jail if you committed a crime was cut by 80%.

(2)

[THERE HAS BEEN a real increase in crime, not just in the number reported]. Overall, 65% of serious crimes were reported in 1981, compared with 67% in 1995 the British Crime Survey has also demonstrated something that most of us know from our own experience: a large proportion of `unreported crimes' are so minor that we would not really regard them as crimes – a short scuffle in a pub, for example ... For offences that are serious enough to warrant a prison sentence, the number of unreported crimes is small.

Even when all kinds of crimes are lumped together, the police and the BCS both tell us that crime rose by 80% between 1981 and 1995. [For earlier years] our best evidence is from people who can remember what life was like in the 1950s. In working-class neighbourhoods ... some people can recall a time when houses were safely left unlocked and bicycles safely left unattended. They remember the shock they felt when someone they knew experienced a crime ... They know that life began to change in the 1960s and 1970s.

(3)

THE ASSERTION that crime rises with wealth is at odds with the facts. During the last half of the 19th century British society underwent one of the most rapid, wrenching transformations from an agricultural to an industrial society that any nation has ever experienced – upheavals of a sort that would lead any modern sociologist to predict a spiralling crime rate. And yet crime dropped.

(4)

WHEN ELIZABETH II came to the throne in 1952 ... crime was falling. There had been a rise in the crime rate through the 1930s and the war years, but it peaked in 1948. Over the next seven years reported crime dropped by 16% in England and Wales. More recently still, from 1993 to 1995, the country abruptly shifted from a steeply rising crime rate to three years of falling overall crime.

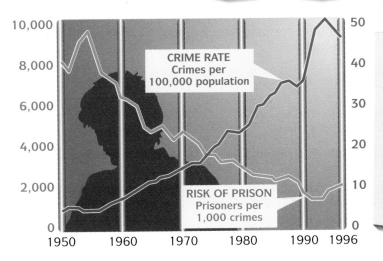

CRIME RATE
Crimes per 100,000 population

RISK OF PRISON
Prisoners per 1,000 crimes

Questions

1 Read Sources **A** and **B**. **a)** Do they suggest that crime is increasing? **b)** What problems do they raise concerning evidence about crime?

2 Can you think of any other difficulties in assessing the extent of crime?

3 Source **F** consists of extracts and illustrations from a newspaper article arguing that we are facing a crime wave caused by the failure to imprison criminals. Read the source carefully and answer the following questions.
   a) What impression of crime is conveyed by the photograph? Is it accurate?
   b) Extract **1** appears to be based on statistical evidence. How statistically valid are its conclusions? How are they reached?
   c) The graph also presents statistics. Can we tell if it is accurate? How is the impression of change affected by the way that the graph is presented?
   d) In the light of Sources **A** to **E**, how reliable are the claims made in extract **2**?
   e) Using your knowledge of nineteenth-century crime and punishment, explain how far extract **3** is accurate in its claims.
   f) Extract **4** points to two periods when crime figures have dropped. What other information would you need in order to assess the significance of this?
   g) The information in this article seems to establish that crime figures have risen and risk of imprisonment fallen. Does this mean that one problem caused the other? Or that there are fewer people in prison?

 Has punishment changed?

Non-custodial punishment

The implication of Source **F** in the previous unit (p. 105) is that crime has risen because punishment is no longer a sufficient deterrent – partly because fewer criminals are caught and convicted, and partly because they are not imprisoned for long enough. Specifically, the author complained about the increasing use of cautions instead of imprisonment for young offenders since 1954.

Fines remain a very common form of punishment – 2 million per year in the 1980s. However, if they are not paid the criminal has to be imprisoned – about a thousand people a year in the 1980s were imprisoned for non-payment (about 3 per cent of the total prison population).

The prison as punishment

At the same time, government reports in recent years have pointed to an explosion in the prison population and serious overcrowding as a result. There have been a number of changes introduced in the last fifty years, many of them intended to encourage rehabilitation of offenders. However, the need for deterrence and retribution, coupled with public resentment when prisoners are perceived as enjoying conditions too good for them, has tended to undermine reform. An example of this alternative approach was the introduction of 'short sharp shock' treatment in 'Boot Camps' by Home Secretary William Whitelaw in the 1980s (see Source **F**).

The sources below illustrate the problems involved in providing effective punishment for a wide variety of offenders and the contradictory results of different initiatives.

Source A Changes in punishment, 1945–82

Year	Change made	Purpose	Applies to
1945	Introduction of open prisons	Allow greater freedom and rehabilitate offenders	Men and women guilty of minor offences
1948	Criminal Justice Act: ended corporal punishment and hard labour	Rehabilitation; fair treatment for offenders	All prison inmates
1948	Criminal Justice Act: brought in extended sentences for frequent offenders	Deterrence and retribution	All adult offenders
1948	Criminal Justice Act: introduced remand centres for juveniles awaiting reports and Detention Centres for 'shock' treatment	Deterrence, and differentiation between new and 'hardened' offenders	All juveniles; male juveniles
1948	Criminal Justice Act: introduced Attendance Centres – local centres for non-custodial treatment of young offenders	Rehabilitation and training; avoiding new offenders learning from older criminals as they tended to in Borstals	All juveniles
1967	Introduction of suspended sentences	'Second chance' to avoid imprisonment	All offenders
1972	Community Service Orders	Rehabilitation; making punishment useful	All juveniles
1982	Criminal Justice Act: defined purposes of imprisonment; replaced Borstals by Youth Custody	To make prison sentences more rational and flexible; deterrence and protection of the public	Adult offenders; young offenders and juveniles

Source B
Prison numbers in the 1980s

In August 1985 there were 48,145 inmates in prisons in Britain (16 per cent of whom were awaiting trial) compared to 42,200 in 1984, in buildings designed for 39,804. In 1984 the Home Office had forecast 43,000 for 1985 and 49,000 for 1992. The prison population had reached its forecast size seven years earlier than expected ... At Leeds, Oxford and Leicester, the number of prisoners exceeds the capacity of the prisons by 100 per cent.

From R. Whiting, *Crime and Punishment*, 1986

Source C HMP Weare, the controversial prison ship in Portland Harbour which began to receive inmates in 1997. This was an attempt to contain the rapid rise in the prison population caused by government policies of the 1990s.

Source D Reconviction rates

The latest research shows that there is little difference between the reconviction rates of those sent to prison and those given community service or probation orders. Given that the most hardened criminals are sent to prison, it is perhaps surprising that the differences are not greater.

From Cooper, *Viewpoints*

Source E From *Manifesto for Change*, produced by the Prison Governors' Association, 1994

We believe that imprisonment is the punishment and that regimes should be based upon a rehabilitative approach ... It is after all the only way in which prison can work.

Source F John McLeod, journalist, on the 'short, sharp, shock'

In 1979, the then Home Secretary, William Whitelaw, delighted the Conservative Party Conference when he promised detention centres where young criminals would get a 'short, sharp, shock' ... Five years later a Home Office report found the regime had no discernible effect on reconviction. It was made tougher but still had no noticeable effect. The short, sharp, shock was quietly shelved.

From Cooper, *Viewpoints*

Questions

1 What changes have taken place in the methods of punishing criminals since 1950?

2 What evidence suggests that the purpose of punishment is rehabilitation?

3 What evidence suggests that the purpose is deterrence or retribution?

4 Can the same punishments address both aims?

5 What are the main problems involved in the use of prison as a form of punishment?

6 Use your knowledge of crime and punishment to answer these questions: **a)** Is punishment now more effective than in the past? **b)** What other forms of punishment could be used?

Capital punishment

Is there a place for capital punishment in modern Britain?

One of the most controversial changes in punishment since the Second World War has been the abolition of the death penalty in 1965. Several attempts have been made to persuade parliament to vote for its restoration. Recent surveys of public opinion suggest that around 80 per cent of the public believe that it should be available as a punishment, but MPs have consistently voted against it.

There are many arguments both for and against capital punishment, some of which are summarised in Source **B**. Probably the two most crucial issues involved are whether or not the death sentence acts as a deterrent, and the risk of making mistakes. Read the sources in this unit, and use them in the context of your knowledge of crime and punishment in the past to answer the questions at the end and to put forward your own view.

Source C Ruth Ellis, the last woman to be hanged in Britain (1956). She was found guilty of killing her lover in a 'crime of passion'.

Source A The 1957 Homicide Act

The Homicide Act of 1957 divided murders into two categories: (a) capital; (b) non-capital. Capital covered killing during theft, avoiding arrest, killing a policeman or prison officer and any second murder. All other killings were classed as non-capital. This arrangement proved very unsatisfactory. The act also brought in the idea of diminished responsibility, meaning a person could not be convicted of murder if suffering from an abnormality of mind at the time of the crime.

From R. Whiting, *Crime and Punishment*, 1986

Source B Arguments for and against hanging

For:
1. A dead murderer cannot kill again.
2. It will deter other people.
3. It will save the money spent on a prisoner during life imprisonment.
4. Most people want to see murderers hanged.
5. Hanging satisfies the victim's relatives.

Against:
1. The wrong person might be hanged.
2. It is not a deterrent, as statistics show.
3. It is against the teachings of different religions.
4. Even the worst person might be reformed.
5. The murderer may be mentally ill or have committed a domestic murder and will never kill again.

From R. Whiting, *Crime and Punishment*, 1986

Source D The death penalty in America

For the rules to be obeyed, they must be accompanied by a sanction that fits the crime ... [The death penalty] is a legitimate expression of moral indignation, a notice that certain acts are simply unacceptable.

G.L. McDowell, Professor of American Studies, University of London

Source E The electric chair is used in America for execution, along with hanging, lethal injection, firing squad and gassing. No method is painless.

Source F The Murder Act, 1965

The Murder (Abolition of Death Penalty) Act in 1965 made life imprisonment the alternative to hanging except for treason and violent piracy ... In the 1970s the prison population increased by 150 murderers a year who were serving life sentences.

From R. Whiting, *Crime and Punishment*, 1986

Source G The view of Albert Pierrepoint, Britain's hangman for twenty-five years

I do not believe that any one of the hundreds of executions I carried out has in any way acted as a deterrent against future murder. Capital punishment n my view achieved nothing except revenge.

Source H Timothy Evans was accused of the murder of his daughter in 1950. In 1966 he was cleared of the crime because of unreliable evidence. It was too late: Evans had been hanged for the murder.

Questions

1 What steps were taken before 1969 to make the use of the death penalty more selective?

2 Why do you think these arrangements proved unsatisfactory?

3 Use the sources and your own wider knowledge to decide: **a)** Does the death sentence act as a deterrent to crime? **b)** Is it possible to guarantee that no mistakes will be made?

4 What are the main arguments for and against the use of the death penalty for:
   • the murder of police or prison officers;
   • murder in pursuit of crime, such as robbery;
   • terrorist murder?

5 Should the death penalty be used for anything other than murder?

6 Is there any evidence to suggest that the existence of the death penalty might make criminals more violent?

7 Using the evidence in the sources and your own knowledge, write a letter to your MP in favour of, or against, the restoration of the death penalty.

Policing in modern Britain

 How far has policing changed since 1950?

The years since the Second World War have seen significant changes in the methods and role of the police, as well as changes in public perceptions of them. On the one hand, police technology and methods used to detect crime have changed radically. This has led to many successes. A particularly useful development has been DNA 'fingerprinting', which has led to arrests in several rape and murder cases.

At the same time, however, complaints about the police have increased and public perceptions of them are very mixed. There have been accusations of racism, corruption, police brutality and simple inefficiency.

The sources in this unit illustrate some of the changes as well as the problems faced by the police. They look at police work in relation to four areas: serious crime, street offences and minor crime, maintaining public order, and relations with the community. Measures have been introduced to improve police work in all of these areas, but they can sometimes be contradictory. For example, the use of cars makes the police more mobile and more able to respond quickly to crimes, but it has also, by taking them off 'the beat', made it more difficult for policemen to know and be known by their communities.

In the light of these sources, you should be able to make some judgements about how far the police have changed, for the better or for the worse, and to what extent their job has simply become more difficult.

Source A Vivien Stern, of the National Association for the Care and Resettlement of Offenders, on black people and the criminal justice system

The evidence strongly indicates that black people are unfairly treated by our criminal justice system. The figures do not show that they are more prone to crime than white people, but they do suggest that black people who offend are twice as likely to be sent to prison.

Source B Lord Scarman in his report into the Brixton riots of 1981

In a materialistic society, the relative ... deprivation it entails is keenly felt, and idleness gives time for resentment and envy to grow. Many of these difficulties face white as well as black youngsters, but it is clear that they bear particularly heavy on young blacks who face the burden of discrimination.

Source C From the *Daily Telegraph*, 25 July 1997

An attempt to hold a police identity parade with blacked-up white men standing alongside a black suspect was described by a judge as 'a farce'. Police in Doncaster were unable to find enough suitable black men to stand beside Martin Kamara. Instead they brought in a make-up artist to change the colour of eight white men.

Source D From *The Times*, 1997

The parents of murdered black teenager Stephen Lawrence brought an unsuccessful private prosecution after police and prosecution authorities failed to secure a conviction, despite identifying the men involved.

Source E Police weapons

The weapons available to the police in case of a breakdown of law and order include electrified water jets, barbed contacts, dart guns, rubber bullets and sound curdlers. Although the Metropolitan Police acquired water cannon in the 1980s, they have not used them because the jets of water can hurl debris from the ground at people and injure them.

From R. Whiting, *Crime and Punishment*, 1986

Source F Examples of police specialisation

Date	Branch/specialised service set up
1758	Mounted police
1798	River police
1877	Criminal Investigation Department (CID)
1883	Special Branch, Metropolitan Police
1901	Fingerprints Branch, Scotland Yard
1935	Forensic Science Laboratory, Hendon
1968	Community Relations Branch
1970	Anti-Terrorist Squad
1980	Air Support Unit

Source G From *The Times*, 17 June 1997

In the past decade cases of wrongful imprisonment have been front-page news. But when Justice – the all-party human rights group – began its work 40 years ago, miscarriages of justice were not acknowledged. The legal establishment failed to recognise that the police – for the best of motives – could fabricate evidence; that the courts could get it wrong.

Source H From *The Times*, 25 July 1997

A black left-wing sociology lecturer was told yesterday by an industrial tribunal that her passionate beliefs had made her see a racist conspiracy where none existed. Ruth Chigwada-Bailey had a claim for racial discrimination dismissed because there was no case to answer. Jessica Hill, the tribunal chairwoman, told Mrs Chigwada-Bailey that she had lost touch with reality and her judgement had been clouded by her feminist and anti-racist beliefs ... and saw a conspiracy of racism in the most innocent remarks at the drugs clinic where she worked.

Source I Policing public meetings

Policing of large public meetings has also changed; in the 1980s football hooliganism was a serious and dangerous problem, and the scenes during the 1984/5 miners' strike echoed disturbances in the 19th century.

From J.M. Coutts et al., *Social Issues*, 1985

Source J How policemen have to dress to carry out their duties in safety at civil disturbances in the 1990s

Questions

1 What duties have the police been expected to carry out since 1950?

2 What changes have there been in police methods?

3 What evidence suggests that new technology has helped policing?

4 What problems has it caused?

5 What complaints have been made about the police in recent years?

6 How have perceptions of the police changed since the 1950s?

7 With reference to policing in the nineteenth century, explain how far these problems are new.

8 In what ways has policing become more difficult since 1950?

9 How have the police responded to these problems?

10 Do you think that policing has got better or worse: **a)** since 1950? **b)** since 1850?

Index

Alfred the Great 24, 26
Anglo-Saxon law and society 22, 24–6
Approved Schools 93
assizes 30, 42, 44

beggars 46–7
benefit of clergy 34, 66
Bentham, Jeremy 78, 82, 88
Bloody Assizes 64–5
Bloody Code 41, 72–3, 88
Bloody Sunday (1887) 85
Borstals 93
Boudicca 19–21
Bow Street Runners 78–9
Bridewell 48
Butler, Josephine 95

capital punishment (see death penalty)
Catholics 40, 42, 44, 52, 54–9, 61, 63, 74,
    101
Chartists 84
Christians, persecution of 18
Church and the law 34–5, 40, 54–7, 61, 63
church courts 34, 45, 60
Cicero 13, 18
CID (Criminal Investigation Department)
    81
Civil War, English 41, 52, 57, 60, 62, 63,
    64, 65
class and the law 9, 10, 17, 18, 23, 41, 46, 64,
    67, 68–9, 72, 74, 76, 80, 83, 84, 86–7, 100
Colquhoun, Patrick 72
common law 30, 43
coroner 32, 33
courts leet 27, 32

Davison, Emily 98, 99
death penalty 4, 14, 15, 16, 17, 26, 31, 48,
    51, 60, 66, 72–3, 78, 100, 108–9
debt, debtors 4, 10, 11, 14, 33, 50
deterrence 33, 69, 91, 106, 108
Dissent, Protestant 63, 65, 66

Elizabeth I 56–7, 60
Ellis, Ruth 108
enclosures 40, 46, 74
Evans, Timothy 109
eyre 30

Fawkes, Guy 57, 58–9
Fenians 81
feudal system 23
Fielding, Henry 66, 70, 72, 73
fingerprinting 87, 110
frankpledge 27
French Revolution 41, 75
Fry, Elizabeth 89

gaols (see prisons)
Gaule, John 61, 62
Gloucester prison 89, 92
Godfrey, Sir Edmund 52–3
Gordon Riots 57, 74
Gunpowder Plot 57, 58–9

Hammurabi 4
Henry II 30–31, 32

Henry VIII 41, 42, 43, 54–5, 60
heresy, heretics 35, 51, 54, 55
highwaymen 41, 53, 87
Hogarth, William 70, 73
honour courts 27, 32
Hopkins, Matthew 62
houses of correction 48, 49
Howard League for Penal Reform 88
hundred courts 25, 27, 30, 32
Hunt, Henry 76–7

Industrial Revolution 41, 68, 93

Jacobite Rebellions 65
James I 40, 43, 57, 58–9
Jarrow March 85
Jeffries, Judge 64
juries 12, 18, 30–31, 32, 43, 66, 78
justice of the peace (JP) 32, 40, 44, 45,
    49, 66, 74, 75
Justinian 10, 13
juveniles and the law (see youth and the
    law)

Lee, Rowland 43
Levellers 50, 64
Lollards 35, 54
London 50–53, 69, 78, 86
London Corresponding Society 75
lord's court 27, 32
Luddites 75, 76
Lytton, Lady Constance 97

Magna Carta 32, 34, 36
manor (manorial) courts 27, 32, 37, 45
Marcher lords 43
Mary, Queen of Scots 56, 57
Mary Tudor 55
media and crime 104–5
Metropolitan Police 78–81
Millbank prison 92
Monmouth Rebellion 64–5
Monteagle, Lord 57, 58–9
More, Sir Thomas 54–5
Moses 5

Naylor, James 63
Newgate prison 52, 53, 89
Nonconformists 63
Norman law and society 23, 27–9

ordeals 26

Pankhurst, Emmeline 96
Parkhurst prison 93
Paul, Sir George 88, 89, 92
Peasants' Revolt 37, 38–9, 54, 64
Peel, Sir Robert 67, 72, 78
peine fort et dure 31
Pentonville prison 92
Peterloo Massacre 76–7, 84
Pilgrimage of Grace 55, 64, 65
pillory 33
Place, Francis 76, 84
poaching 41, 67
police, policing 75, 78–85, 101, 110–11
poll tax 28–9, 101

poor laws 40, 48–9, 50
praetor 11, 12
prerogative courts 40, 42–3
prisons 18, 30, 33, 34, 50, 53, 78, 79,
    88–9, 91–3, 104–5, 106–7
prostitution 94, 95
Protestants 40, 42, 54, 56, 61, 63, 65, 66
Puritans 42, 56, 61, 63, 64

Quakers 63

race and the law 9, 18, 19–21, 101, 102,
    103, 110, 111
Rebecca Riots 84
rebellions (see riots and rebellions)
Reformation 42, 54–5, 61
rehabilitation 69, 91, 106, 107
retribution 33, 69, 91, 106
Richard II 28–9
Riot Act 84
riots and rebellions 7, 19–20, 23, 38–9,
    40, 47, 52, 55, 57, 64–5, 74–5, 76–7, 84–5
Roman Britain 19–21
Romans, Rome 6–21
Romilly, Sir Samuel 78

Savundra, Emil 103
Saxon law and society (see Anglo–Saxon
    law and society)
Separate System 91–2
Separatists 63, 64
Sheppard, Jack 53
sheriff 25, 27, 32, 42, 44
shire courts 25, 27, 30, 33
Silent System 91–2
smuggling 41, 67
socio–political crime 67
Star Chamber 42
stocks 33, 35
Suffragettes 95, 96–9
Suffragists 96

technology 69, 86–7, 100
Ten Commandments 4–5
terrorism 101
tithing 25, 32
transportation 41, 66, 73, 90
trial by battle 28–9
Turpin, Dick 53
Twelve Tables 10, 14–15, 17
Tyler, Wat 38–9

Union, Acts of 40, 43

vagabonds, vagrancy 47, 48, 49, 50, 66, 93

Wake, Kidd 75
Weare, HMP 107
wergild 24
Wild, Jonathan 53
William I 23, 27, 28, 34
witchcraft, witches 60–62
women and the law 15, 16, 25, 34, 35,
    60–62, 89, 94–9
Wormwood Scrubs 91

youth and the law 73, 93, 106–7